T0130147

The Unapologetic Quest For Success

Order this book online at www.trafford.com
or email orders@trafford.com

Most Trafford titles are also available at major online book retailers.

This book is non-fictional. With a few exceptions, names
have been changed to protect the identities of the characters.

ISBN: 978-1-4269-2553-5 (sc)
ISBN: 978-1-4269-2554-2 (dj)
ISBN: 978-1-4269-2552-8 (e)

*Our mission is to efficiently provide the world's finest, most comprehensive book publishing
service, enabling every author to experience success. To find out how to publish your book,
your way, and have it available worldwide, visit us online at www.trafford.com*

Trafford rev. 2/12/2010

 www.trafford.com

North America & international
toll-free: 1 888 232 4444 (USA & Canada)
phone: 250 383 6864 ♦ fax: 812 355 4082

CONTENTS

Disclaimer

This book is non-fictional. With a few exceptions, names have been changed to protect the identities of the characters.

Inspiration For The Book

The inspiration for the book was taken from "I can do all things through Christ who strengtheneth me" Philippians chp4 v:13

I keep remembering my mom saying, "Seek knowledge, wisdom and understanding in life, develop a connection with your inner spirit, never ask for silver or gold and maintain a philosophy of love. Love for God, love for your neighbour. If you cannot be grateful to your neighbour you can see, you cannot be grateful to God whom you cannot see. Love is like a well; the more you extract from it the purer and cleaner it remains. All forces on earth operate in harmony and love". In the quest for success one always has to give back. This publication is geared to provide insights, experiences and knowledge of a medical doctor in his "Quest for Success" (from Hairoun to Cuba and back!).

Dedications

This book is dedicated to my deceased parents, my mom Lucy Alexandrina Toney née Layne and my father James Fitzgerald Toney. You are my greatest exemplars of generosity, love, hope, faith and human dignity.

Special dedication to my brothers and sisters, Cephus 'Adrian' Toney, Theresa 'Debbie' Toney, James 'Elvis' Toney and Sharon 'Nicole' John. Your unwavering support for the entire project during my sojourn to Cuba and back is unmatched by anyone except mom. I thank the Lord that he gave me such wonderful brothers and sisters.

To Usain Bolt, Oprah Winfrey, Rosa Parks and Barack Obama, you have re-energized my inner being to contribute to the upliftment of humanity.

To Spike Lee and Tyler Perry. You have given hope to black entertainers world wide.

To Jennifer Williams my fiancée for your love and also your invaluable support in caring for Chester Jr. and Jé-vonni throughout my busy schedule at the office and writing and producing this book.

To Chester Jr. I am thrilled by your sense of humor and I am happy to call you my son. I know you will make an impact on the world by God's grace. You are such a wonderful child.

To Jé-vonni my son (not biologically), reach for the highest heights and let no one tell you it cannot be done.

To the nation of St. Vincent and the Grenadines on its 30th anniversary of its independence.

To the Cuban people in their continuous struggle for self-determination and social justice.

Acknowledgement

Arthur Bobb, Renwick Rose, Justice Adrian Saunders, Rev. Oscar Allen, Corbett Crick, Luenda Johnson, Hugh Drakes (deceased), Julian Jack (Accountant), Julian Jack (Attorney-at-Law), Diana Bailey, Gerald Williams, Elroy 'Blaze' Findlay, Dr. Franklyn James, Dr. Maurice Robertson, Dr. Ellsworth Charles, Dr. Edmund Sealey, Dr. Fitzgerald Walker, Stanley Browne, Dr. Naale Rose-Morgan, Dr. Joanna Osborne, Cameron Stephens, Winston Soso, Gwendolyn "Soso" Jones, Michael Seales, Dr Heather Hepburn, Cassion Browne, Dr. Estaban Richards, Steve Millington, Val DaSilva, James "Elvis" Toney, Calvin Nichols, Mr. F. I. Jack, Shantel and Marlon Wyllie, Yasmin Adams, Kelly Lewis, Ashford Samuel, Ann Derrick, Dr. Rowena Derrick, Stanley Harris, Ezra Ledger, Augustine Power, Tswala Browne, Godfred Pompey, Sebastien "Bassy" Alexander, Professor José Oliva, Professor Nelson Rodriquez, Mercedes Alimentero (Midwife), Professor Blanca Rosa Manzano, Professor Roberto Roman, Dr. Kenia Hernandez, Dr. Alberto Martinez, Dr. Sergio Parejas, Dr. Mario Calzadilla Cruz, Lotia and Dexter Rose, Dr. Pedro Cassanova, Edelso Moret Darcot, Niurka Menendez, Dr. Eduardo Tamayo, Maria Sanchez, Julian Farrell, Irvin Samuel, Earl "Ole George" Daniel, James Bentinck, Paulo Barnabe, Desmond Dabreo, Tamya Williams, Joe Delves, Wilma Cumberbatch, Marva Murray, Urel "Snake" Seaton, David Bonadie, Dr. Edgar "Doc" Adams, Nekeisha Adams, Bernard Wyllie, Uriel Wyllie, Jerusha Fredricks, Vivian Bonadie (deceased), Vondelon Williams, Leroy Rock, Eduardo Garvey, Elmore Browne, Dr. Collin Boyle, Dr. Bertram Stephens, Bruno Thomas, Varis Lavia, Michel John (Computec), Shryl Thomas, Kozel Williams McAlister, Harriet Richardson, Frank Layne, Dawn Bascombe Richardson, Dr. Christian Anderson, Felix Lavia, Ingerlisa Lavia-Fergusson, Dougal James, Thalia Williams, Jé-vonni Williams, Calvert Craigg, Norris Toney, Orlando Fergusson, Vanette Williams, Jolene Collins, Professor Orlando Mitjans, Lorraine Samuel, Alister Browne, Osmay Luis Rosabald Gonzales, Douglas, Kurt, and Gregory Richards, Conley 'Chivambo' Rose, Rene Ollivierre, Mr. Cleve

Lewis, Hazelanne Mofford-Jones André Robinson, Dr. Douglas Slater and Dr. Sherrian Slater, Carl Browne, Salisha King, Edward Beache, Andrew Simmons, Sonny Peters, Frank George, Bernice Charles, Leah Ollivierre, Andrew Rogers, Ian Rogers, Ricardo Rick Mc Donald, Bella Nadal, Benson Quamina, Steve Collis, 'Con' Joseph, Kenneth Williams and Calvert Bowens.

Production Team

Production Manager and Financier: Dr. Chester Toney

Graphic Design/Layout: Ken Dyer

Typesetting/IT Specialist: Andra Layne

Photographer (front page):   Denzil Sardine

Contributing Photographers: Dave Roberts

Editor: Ercelle Thomas

Other Contributors: Ophesta Stephens

        Cephus Toney

About the Book

This is a true story about Dr. Chester Toney. He takes the readers from birth and early childhood development through his adolescence and early adult life while pursuing a medical career at the University of Havana. He emphasizes his fate upon his return from medical school with a specialist degree in Obstetrics/Gynaecology. He highlights his early struggles as a teenager to overcome social and economic hardships and states his success studying by candle light to complete his secondary education. During the course of the book, he outlines some of his humanitarian activities and gives readers a sneak peek of his love life in Cuba. The Unapologetic Quest for Success (from Hairoun to Cuba and back) outlines how by medically supervising and instructing Earl 'Ole George' Daniel and Joel Butcher in endurance walking, he was able to share in the lime light as a trail blazer in four unofficial world record breaking performances. In a unique way he reveals his love formula for successful relationships through twenty years experience personally and medically. He exposes many of the lessons learnt in dealing with the opposite sex.

He unravels some of his rare encounters in his medical career and shares them in a simple and interesting manner that rivets your attention all the way through. These twelve rare medical pathologies encountered by a Vincentian doctor are very educational and informative and to some extent quite entertaining. He challenges you the reader that you would have never read anything like this before in any medical journal whether past or present. This chapter is a must read. Later he gives readers a glimpse into his next book, "Sex you don't see on TV".

He also shares in an interview with a freelance journalist from St. Vincent and the Grenadines (Neville Thompson) about Cuba, past, present and future and he was able to enunciate his vision for Cuba and St. Vincent and the Grenadines. He expresses gratitude to Fidel Castro and the Cuban people. It is very touching, profound and sincere. Finally he shares in an aspect of his life that not even many of his closest friends know about. This is indeed a secret revealed for the first time, his poetic side. This gives many readers a journey along "The many moods of Dr. Chester Toney".

St. Vincent and the Grenadines and Cuba are the two countries that played a pivotal role in his unapologetic quest for success. This is his way of saying thank you to all who have moulded him up to this day. The unapologetic quest for success is indeed a winner! And I am thankful for the opportunity to be associated with this historic project.

Andra M. Layne, I.T. Specialist – Customs & Excise Dept., St. Vincent and the Grenadines.

The Unapologetic Quest For Success

ABOUT THE AUTHOR

Dr. Chester Linburgh Toney M.D. was born into a humble, working class family in the rural village of Carriere, Marriaqua, St. Vincent and the Grenadines. Both of his parents are deceased.

Conventionally he has pursued post-graduate training in Perinatology, Oncological Surgery in Gynaecology, Urogenital Surgery, Sexology, and Laparoscopy and Infertility.

He is a self-financed Obstetrician/Gynecologist/Sexologist, who studied medicine in the Republic of Cuba, between the years 1987 and 1998. Dr. Chichester Toney M.D. is a graduate of the Manual Fajardo Medical School in Havana and Ramon Gonzalez Corro Obstetrics and Gynaecology Hospital in Cuba.

He has pursued post-graduate studies in Alternative Medicine, under the guidance of Cuban Professor Dr. Gisella Abon Rodriquez, in the following disciplines: Homeopathy, Acupuncture, Shiatsu massage, Electro-Acupuncture, including Chiropractic adjustments, etc. He is also trained in Counseling.

He operates a busy medical practice in capital city, Kingstown, St. Vincent & the Grenadines. He has been practising medicine in his homeland for the last ten (10) years; he is very popular among the under-privileged working class, and alternative medicine enthusiasts.

This is his first published book. He has written many articles on health and sexology in the Searchlight newspaper in St. Vincent and has been a guest on various radio programmes and lectures in his country.

Tribute to Lucy Alexandrina Toney

(1940-2005)

I remember quite vividly, it was August 12th, 2004. I bought a plaque in Brooklyn, New York, for my mom's birthday. I had looked the entire gift shop for a present that reflected very much how I felt about her. I was finally successful with this plaque that read: "Of all the things both great and small a mother's love is best of all." This gift represented my deepest and sincerest feelings for my mom. In fact, it was the epitome of my mother's love and her influences on me that molded my character, my dreams and aspirations, and my deeper spiritual being. It is only when one has fathered or mothered a child that one begins to feel what parenting is really all about. Though it is believed that a father's love is not as profound as a mother's love, I believe it depends on the individual and not so much the gender. The quotation above resonates a lot with me, even years after my mom died, I still believe that love and Mom are synonymous. Mom was no ordinary human being. She had great faith. "I will know the exact moment when I am going to die," she would say even when she was very ill. "Don't worry, I'm not going to die now, the Lord is not ready for me yet, I will know the exact time". She was meticulous, tactful, and highly diplomatic, qualities she attributed to her father who was of Jewish/Scottish descent.

She was always conscious of other people's emotions and tried not to upset them in any hurtful way. She also believed that whatever action an adult takes, he/she must be accountable for it. Mom always said, "Your actions whether good or bad, should be decisions you make on your own and not influenced by other people." This created conflict when she wanted to give advice. In fact, she believed the most important aspect of becoming an adult is making decisions on your own. Being unable to make decisions on your own demonstrates a great sense of immaturity. This philosophy I have adopted during the course of my lifetime, sometimes making unpopular decisions, but at the end, feeling satisfied with myself. Mom repeatedly said, "You have seventy years, if you live that long to make your mark in the world as a unique human being. Only you have that opportunity to do so, that's why you need to develop your own style, and methodology in handling the world, and all the craziness the world has to offer. That is why imitating others is totally unacceptable.

She believed very strongly, that no problem is insurmountable. She believed that ladies were blessed with femininity, which should be nurtured and molded in a positive way, and not in a vulgar manner. Women must reflect an image of love, peace and happiness. When these qualities are combined together, it is very difficult for the average male to resist her attraction. In fact, it softens masculinity. She always reflected after my father died her desire to enter the business world. Surprisingly there was much opposition from her male counterparts who became very rough and crude to her. She reminisced at her plight. Many of them had roughed her up not seeing a man by her side. Others tried to make her their prey, basically making excuses, such as being unable to assist in any business venture, but giving their telephone numbers and suggesting a "friendship". "Beautiful ladies like you, should not be in business," one man said to her. But in her diplomatic way, she responded, "I don't mix business with pleasure, because pleasure is not my business." She alluded to the fact that Oprah Winfrey, a beautiful black woman as she is, never let her beauty be a distraction in her quest to fulfill her dreams of being successful. She was very conscious of the fact that this is a man's world, but it would be nothing without a woman or girl as James Browne says. On numerous occasions, she lectured to young ladies, that a woman must have the charm of a dove and serpent-like qualities to strive, when the time comes, and know how to use them, based on time, circumstances and place, but always to bring some good to herself, her family and humanity. These qualities, she said she adapted from Martin Luther King Jr's. book, "Strength to Love".

Two of my Mom's favourite songs were, "On top of the world" by The Carpenters and "Yesterday", by the Beatles. There were very few persons on the island, who had such in depth knowledge of practical horticulture, as my mom did. In fact, she was one of the first persons in St. Vincent to have started horticulture on a commercial level, some thirty (30) years ago. She had a very wide knowledge of all the tropical varieties of flowers and shrubs that existed on the island, and knew by heart, all the varieties. Not only that, she also knew what type of soil to plant them in, what time of year to plant them, and how to care for them. She was one of the first persons who pointed out to me that plants are sensitive to the surroundings and human emotions, and they grow according to how humans interact with them, a science that is today evolving and becoming popular. She encouraged me to replant trees, especially when one was destroyed, a philosophy which was further solidified by José Marti, Cuban's national hero, who said, "A man must plant a tree, make a child, marry a woman, write a book, and build a house, before he dies". (I wonder how many of us have pursued this philosophy).

Cooking was her passion, followed by interior decoration. However, she had great taste and a flair for fashion, designing dresses and baking munchy cakes. One of the virtues of my mom was that she read widely and had no fear of investing in books. Because of this, she was 'well-versed' on various topics, ranging from history, medicine, music, biology, and agronomy to plumbing.

Her strongest lessons were **"No one is better than you"** and "**You don't measure wealth by how much money you have, but by how many things you have for which you won't take money.**"

She was a "self made professor" according to her friends. She would be remembered as being the first person to have the idea of a "Banana Bank" (an autonomous bank set up and managed by banana farmers that looks after the welfare of banana growers and their families). But this same idea was popularized by Bucky Boyea and even patented as being his own (No hard feelings Bucky!) May your soul rest in peace. She would also be remembered for first having the idea or dream of an environmentally friendly hotel, where nothing goes to waste, everything is recycled. Mom's main vision however, was the building of a modern and well equipped library and a school for the people of Carriere. Long live her memory and progressive ideas.

Preface

"Two books for the price of one! The epic story is the unvarnished truth of the life history of a rural boy of genuinely "humble" beginning; who survived some of the most atrocious and devious events of life struggles, including a most heinous attempt of homicide against the lives of his entire family; but who still grew up to become a medical doctor associated with international record breaking fame, thus becoming one of the most illustrious and popular icons in his country.

The Unapologetic quest for success is a read for all; however it is the fervent wish of the author that this story will serve as an inspiration beacon for all those youths who would share similar life experiences to his.

The book is an emotion-packed read. Despite the authentic nature of the story the contents of its chapters are pregnant with the sort of excitements and mood swings that I am sure would keep its readers glued to its pages. His poetic side complements the story but also brings out the deeper thoughts of the author. A must read! – Ardon Nelson, poet, song writer, literary and performing arts critic, consultant in urban planning, St. Vincent and the Grenadines

"A book with a difference. Twenty (20) years ahead of its time!" – Dr. Edmund Sealey, Former Chiropractor of the Victorious West Indies Cricket Team of the 80's

These two reviews have humbled me tremendously, especially coming from two dispassionate and fierce literary critics. They have also enabled me a greater understanding that my objectives of writing an interesting book have been mostly achieved. I must reiterate that I did not write a perfect book as you the readers will conclude after you have dissected and desecrated my writings. I wrote a book which I consider to be simple and different from all other books I've read in the past. A book that is unique in style and content, a book that stresses the success of man biologically, socially and spiritually. There are no shortcuts to success unless you are planning to be dishonest in your quest.

I believe, no I don't believe, I know I have written an interesting book. I am not blowing my own trumpet, but if I don't think so, why should you? I have written a true story that resonates with many of you, the readers. I hope that I may be able to touch many lives in a positive way. I also believe that I can give hope to those who despair and share the passion of unwavering perseverance with those who are suffering.

I have decided to write this book based on human suffering, trials and tribulation, and my quest to escape poverty by grabbing an education. In such a harsh and competitive world, the experiences and revelations in this book are usually frank and full of my resistance against formidable odds. They reflect my victories, my pursuit to do good, not evil and my dreams and aspirations.

My mom once highlighted to me that the cemeteries are some of the richest places on earth because they are filled with so many persons who had great dreams that never materialized. I did not want to fall into that unfortunate group of persons. It was imperative that I write this book before that time arrives; for if I didn't, the world would have missed a golden opportunity to know me.

I am still humbled by the words of one of my Cuban ex-girlfriends who always asked, "How can such a small island as St. Vincent and the Grenadines nurture and develop such a wonderful and unique human being?" It's always touching to have a close friend saying positive things about you when others are saying differently. I have always thought that my life story will make a prolific best seller. It is rare, inspirational, deeply spiritual, unapologetically humane, humble, touching and connects with the poor and unfortunate, the working class and the under-privileged. Most of all it shows how to stay focused under some of the most trying and extreme circumstances.

My life reflects a constant battle to overcome adversity, some of my own making but all in the struggle to do good and assist the poor and the needy. Greed and the lack of human gratitude raised its ugly head trying to hinder my quest for success from becoming a reality. To those who were involved in this saga, "Ingratitude is worse than witchcraft."

This book is destined to become a bestseller and like any great work of art, it is surrounded by glorious uncertainties and numerous controversies. If I had not envisaged it becoming a best seller, I would not have written it in the first place. If I had thought otherwise, I definitely would not have started. Mind you I did not write this book purely for fame and fortune nor material prosperity. I did so because I was inspired by the vision of how a country boy can come to capital Kingstown to seek an education and in so doing be granted the opportunity to study in a foreign country and survive conditions of war in times of peace for eleven years. I excelled with flying colours then returned to my homeland where my ambition became too large for the status quo, therefore I was kept outside the system. I transcended treacherous circumstances to become catapulted to stardom as a four time world record breaking physician; this is a story worth reading. Additionally, I became a prolific struggler against injustice, adversities and oppression. The struggle never stops. It has only just begun. This book is an ideal collector's item. Happy reading! To God be the Glory! Praise the Lord!

Chapter 1

A Country Boy – Chester Toney

I was born on 31st December 1968 at 10:00 p.m. in the rural village of Carriere in the Marriaqua Valley. I can only imagine my mom that night of the delivery of her third child Chichester Lindburgh Toney. In those days there was no ultrasound, so the sex of the fetus was not known before delivery. The local folklore had many different ways to determine the sex; many at times spot on target. According to tradition, I was already adjudged a boy so there was no mistake. My great aunt Esther must have been overjoyed, and I can only visualize her shouting, "Lucy, it's a boy!" I was told that I weighed 8lbs 1oz when I was born and was very pink. My great aunt Esther was very instrumental in making sure that my mom had a safe delivery as she was the well-experienced mid-wife for the Marriaqua valley. From then onwards she has always been close to me even up to today. Aunty Esther was the daughter of "Old Browne" my step great grandfather on my mother's side, and Anna 'Neyna' Simon, my great grandmother and this marriage produced eight children. Percival Layne (my grandfather) was related to the Layne family, who own one of the oldest businesses in Kingstown. The story has been told that my great grandmother Neyna was a beautiful fair-skinned lady of Carib descendants who went to work with the Laynes in Prospect. Mr. Layne is reported to have said that she was the finest woman he had ever set eyes on. He could not resist this beauty and the rest is history.

They produced one son (Percival) from that relationship which was my grandfather who at 6ft 4ins was dubbed one of the most handsome Vincentian men of his time. He lived with the Layne family until he was ten years old when 'Old Browne' married Neyna and insisted that she reclaim her son. The story has been told that my grandfather Percival

Layne came to Carriere riding on a horse. From that day onwards, he was one of the most sought after young men in the community. He developed into a fine all-rounder, woodcutter, carpenter, mason and builder. He was an expert in rearing animals, especially cows. Many older persons in the village still comment that the best cattle that they ever saw were those reared by him, including one bull they referred to as 'Whitey' which was about 5ft 7inches tall. People came from all parts of the island to get a glimpse of this gigantic bull. My grandfather was from a very large family. He was the first of eight children. They were Uncle Lawrence Browne (deceased), Uncle Peter Browne (deceased), Uncle Cardon Browne (deceased), Uncle Roy Browne (deceased), Uncle Robert Browne, Aunt Aida Browne (deceased), Aunt Kate Browne-Marks and Aunt Esther Browne. My grandmother on my mother's side was Euna Williams of Welcome Village. I was told that her mother was born a slave and her name was Hessey Williams. (I did not get to know her; she died before I was born.) On my father's side of the family, my father James 'Jimmy" Toney was the son of Cephus Toney who spent many years working in the oil fields of Aruba during the 1940's and early 50's. His mother Mabel Glasgow of Sharpes had four children including my father. They were Cora Jack, Ainsley Glasgow, Kenneth Glasgow and Mary Glasgow (deceased). I am very close to Aunty Cora and her eight children, Kurt, Gregory, Dougie, Roger, Donna, Alana, Julia and Junior. Also on my father's side is my cousin Festus Toney and cousin Milton Mayers (deceased). I was christened at the Catholic Church in Mesopotamia with the name Chichester Lindburgh Toney, a name given to me by my father upon birth. However, upon registering this name at the registry, an error was made and Cichester was entered. This was never corrected by an affidavit, so my real name Chichester was never recorded on my birth certificate and that's how it stayed up to this day.

You may ask, what's in a name? You see, my father intentionally gave me this name because of its relevance and significance to him. He believed that a man's names should reflect his character, personality and also his aspirations. My great aunt Esther and my mom adhered to family tradition and immediately buried the placenta and umbilical cord (colloquially called the Navel String) in the backyard garden. I have marked the exact spot with incredible precision. In fact, all my other siblings' navel strings were buried there too. They were buried in the root of a collection of Gros Michel banana trees. It is interesting to note that my son Chester Jr had a piece of his umbilical cord buried there too. This represents the physical bonding of father and son from the same roots and by extension the village of Carriere and ultimately St. Vincent and the Grenadines.

Carriere is known to be a fine producer of bananas and other root crops. For those of you who don't know, St. Vincent and the Grenadines was once called Yurumein and later Hairoun by the Caribs. The name St. Vincent was given to the land because it was said to be discovered by Christopher Columbus on Saint Vincent's Day (and named after a Spanish saint). However, many scholars and historians such as Dr. Edgar Adams and Dr. Adrian Fraser now produce evidence to confirm that Christopher Columbus could not have discovered the island at the time he said he did. That's a very long story that I wouldn't like to get into now.

My dad (James Toney) had a passion for airplanes, aeronautics, circumnavigation of the world etc. Sir Francis Chichester was the first person to circumnavigate the globe by sea and he did so with his dog, and Linburgh was also the first to do so by airplane. My mom also reiterated that dad always ensured that he gave his children great names for if they did not become great, he was not to be blamed as he had given them the right start – great names.

I cherish and hold dearly to my heart the early episodes of my father's discipline, great smile and affection. I miss daddy and sometimes regret that he did not live to see his dreams become reality. Nevertheless, I'm still grateful today for his strong influences on my life in honesty, discipline, love for humanity, love for my country and love for God. Dad had worked in the gold mines in British Guyana in the late 50's. He loved Guyana very much and had travelled to many different countries around the world. Some of his close friends have related to me that before he died, dad told them that on his tombstone he would like the epitaph to be written, James Toney, Vincentian to the bone; travelled the world, loved his family and friends and died in St. Vincent and the Grenadines.

He really loved his homeland St. Vincent and the Grenadines. I guess it could be said like father like son. Daddy must be smiling now up in heaven to see his third child write such positive things about him. Many who knew him will say that he was deeply opinionated and decisive and had a sixth sense for creating profit from any business venture. One person described him as having prolific business acumen. He was an avid businessman who saw profit in any business he planned to undertake. He never tried to exploit anyone. He believed that when you took from the poor, you should give the poor something in return.

He was unlike the average businessman whose only concern was profit by any means necessary and neglecting customer service, civic duties and social work. He was never ruthless in his quest for success and lived by the philosophy that what you give comes back to you, your children and grandchildren. In fact, dad's philosophical and progressive outlook of life made him declare one day to my mom, 'Chichester will be a great man one day and would make the village of Carriere proud in years to come.' I am still anticipating that day.

James Toney was a household name in Carriere village. His nickname 'More land' was given to him because of his unbending philosophy that there was always more land undiscovered in the west.

Daddy never fell short of promises to his children. It was unfortunate and deeply regrettable that he went to the great beyond when I was just three years old. There are a few things that I distinctly remember about him even at the tender age of three. One such thing is that he walked around the house in socks and slippers. He was very hairy skinned and I would pull the hair on his chest while playing with him. I would ask my mom repeatedly at that age, why God had to take him away from us so soon, and she always replied that God had more useful things for him to do in heaven than on earth. I'll always remember her saying, "The Lord giveth and the Lord taketh away, never question why, only God knows why!"

Daddy's death has left an indelible effect upon me. The tenacious memories of him still linger incessantly in my mind. It is said that he lived a full life by virtue of his success in business. He had achieved many material possessions namely, trucks, buses, cars, lands and real estate. He was in fact one of the first Vincentians who had ever owned a convertible Triumph sports car on the island in the early 60's. At that time it is said that he drove a bus in the morning, a truck during the day, a bus again in the evening and a car at night. Daddy was very meticulous in the way he handled his responsibilities as a bus driver, being cognizant of the fact that people's lives were always in his hands. He was always polite and conscious of the needs of his passengers. It is said it was a pleasure to travel with him from Carriere to Kingstown and back, Monday to Saturday. Many bus drivers have said that my father's record of being the most generous bus driver in St. Vincent is still unsurpassed. On Fridays and at month ends, he bought popsicles, ice-cream and snow-cones for his customers who travelled with him regularly.

Dad's generosity had touched the heart of Mr. Vivian Bonadie (Entrepreneur and founder of Bonadie's Ltd) so profoundly that the day I approached him to rent a space for my clinic, he asked, "You are Jimmy's son?" I replied respectfully, "Yes Mr. Bonadie." He said, "Well I really don't have a space, but because you are Jimmy's son and Jimmy was very good to me in the days when I was creeping in business, I must find a space for you. I will have to discuss this with the other members of the company. Don't despair though, I will try my best to convince them. Your father was very good to me and he was one of the few persons I ever trusted with all my heart in this world. I was very saddened to hear of his death, in fact my family and I went to the funeral. It was a pity he died so early. One thing I can tell you is that if he had lived longer he would have been a very powerful businessman in this country. It is because of your father's good deeds that I am considering you. If you are Jimmy Toney's son you too must be a good person. After all the fruit doesn't fall too far from the tree."

Suddenly it struck me that this was what my father meant by doing good deeds. Mr. Bonadie reminded me that dad wasn't an easy man to go with, he had "talks'. "He used to tell me his children were born to be professionals. He said that he would work the clothes off his back to ensure this happened." "I'm so glad that his dreams came true," Mr. Bonadie added. "He helped me a lot when I was just starting in business. He transported lots of sand, cement and other construction materials for me in the earlier days, sometimes free of charge. Now it's my turn to help him by helping you. He used to joke a lot with me and reiterated on numerous occasions that we are two of the luckiest men in the world. We have health, some wealth and two of the most beautiful and honest women in the world. Oh how your dad made me laugh, he was so much fun."

After my dad died at the age of 36 in 1972 of a ruptured aneurysm in the brain, many persons came forward making claims for debts owing to them by him. Some of their claims were just imaginary as there was no proof most of the time. Many unscrupulous persons made fraudulent claims, falsifying documents with bogus signatures for debts and compensation. Dad's death represented a whole new awakening for the family. It also unfolded as one of the most testing periods for my mom. She had to undergo much stress and defamatory abuse and even threats to her life on her husband's behalf. To add insult to injury, some very callous persons chopped down our entire banana plantation and maliciously destroyed all the produce that we had cultivated. Our livestock were poisoned and stolen. I can recall my mom crying and asking the Lord for faith to handle these trials and tribulations and to change the hearts of such devious men.

Next in line were the vehicles. Many of his friends came to my mom stating that they had helped my father buy these vehicles, wanting to assume ownership by some false means. Mom was living a virtual nightmare; I cried profusely seeing her in this dilemma. To compound this dismal situation, our family home was razed to the ground by spiteful and ungodly men. Can you imagine lighting the family home with four children inside and making sure that all the doors were locked so that we couldn't escape the inferno? By some miracle we escaped through a window onto a scaffold on the outside of the house assisted by our adopted brother McKen Woods-Baptiste now deceased (may God rest his soul). The smell of smoke or clothes burning sometimes reminds me of that dreadful day. We almost lost our lives. Thanks to many helpful neighbours and persons like my cousin John Browne, we were able to salvage some possessions and prevent the house from burning completely.

Mom could have thrown up her hands in defeat or she could have lost her mind, but she clung to her faith and remained resolute in the belief that the Lord would see her through. We survived the ordeal.

'Lord, show me my friends for I know you will take care of my enemies for me.'

Ophesta Stephens – unpublished poet

Chapter 2

Mom I do love you

Lucy Alexandrina Toney nee Layne was my mom. She was the only child resulting from the marriage of Percival Layne and Euna Williams. My mom had only two more known sisters, Joletta John of Collins and Rita Layne of Riley. She never had any brothers unfortunately. She always yearned for a brother, but I guess that in life you do not get all you yearn for.

I'm very close to all of Aunt Rita's children and also to Josel John, the daughter of my aunt Joletta. My aunt Rita has seven children namely, Randolph Layne, Cecelia Layne-George, Debra Layne, Francis Layne, Desmarie Layne, Bernard Layne and Andrew Layne. Andra Layne who is actually the typesetter and IT Specialist for 'The Unapologetic Quest for Success' was trained in London and Japan and is the daughter of Cecelia Layne-George.

My mom devoted a lot of time to inculcating a sense of responsibility, love, respect and determination in all her children. Being a young widow with four young children, she imparted strong morals and spiritual values to her family. She will always be remembered "as the mother who fathered me". Having performed the duties of dad and mom meant that some adjustments had to be made in her personality and modus operandi. It meant that it was no longer business as usual and her family had to be balanced with some dose of masculinity, especially to guide and protect her three restless young boys.

She adjusted quickly to her new role. Her role as manager of dad's indebted estate was paramount in protecting her interests and material possessions left behind by my dad. She was now an apprentice in practical business administration. She had an insatiable appetite to succeed. She learnt quickly on the job and set out to take control and eradicate all debts owing on the assets left behind, also her own assets that were now one through the union of marriage. She wrestled with taking care of four very young children, refinancing her new business which included selling parts for vehicles, cultivating the lands and animal husbandry.

From a tender age, I learned quickly about vehicles and their parts. I knew what was a radiator, a distributor, a crank shaft and differential. I also learnt a lot about the rearing of animals and it was then I got my first real experience in delivering goats, sheep and cows. I guess that's where my first interest in Obstetrics and Gynaecology was born. As a young lad growing up in the country side, I learnt a lot about alternative medicine, for example using the leaves of 'Jumbie Soursop' today called Noni, for muscular skeletal pains and arthritis by heating them with olive oil and placing them on the affected area with a bandage. Trumpet Bush for a cold. Cudjoe Root for tumors, whether malignant or benign. Neem Bush for diabetes and hypertension, Lemon (whole) puree for female menstrual disorder and discharge, and stinging nettle for prostate problems. All these we learnt from traditional medicine; so you see where my gravitation to alternative medicine began.

Mom left a legacy in banana cultivation in St. Vincent and the Grenadines. She was one of the first female major producers of the fruit on a large scale and also she was one of the largest employers of agricultural workers in the Marriaqua Valley. This will surprise you. She had the original idea to organize and establish a banana bank. This project was popularized by the now deceased Bucky Boyea, may his soul rest in peace. She was very open minded and opposed injustice everywhere. She left another legacy in religion in St. Vincent and the Grenadines. I know Pastor Errol Daniel and his congregation are very thankful to her for giving up part of her home to conduct church services in the initial stages and before they finally established their own church at Carriere. Pastor Errol Daniel and his small congregation at that time journeyed to Carriere to attend church services which were held at our home. She gave Pastor Daniel full accommodation- benches, chairs, tables and parking space. All this was provided free of cost. No rent was collected for the use of the facilities for many years.

Church was held on various days of the week, but Sunday worship was the main activity. She would go down in the history of the Streams of Power church as playing a pivotal role in laying the foundation for the construction of the church at Carriere. But mom as humble as she has always been said frequently, "To God be the Glory. I am just mortal and imperfect, and the Lord used me as an instrument to establish his church; I claim no honour."

Mom always wanted the best for her children so therefore when it was time for us to attend primary school she chose the most reputable private primary school, Petersville Primary School run by the Peters family both mother and daughter. My brother Elvis (James), Sister Debbie (Theresa) and I had to wake up at 4:30 each morning to prepare for school. We had to walk about 2 miles from Carriere to Green Corner (in La Croix) to catch a bus going to Kingstown for 7:00a.m. Very often we had to walk from the main bus stop to the school up hilly terrain which was almost another mile.

I spent the formative years of my primary education at the Petersville Primary School between 1973 and 1980. It was a whole new world, new friends, new environment and a new education. I adjusted to the situation remarkably well. My grades were favorably consistent throughout. Then I got a skip in class from Junior 2 to Junior 4. The other years of my schooling at Petersville consisted of preparations for the Common Entrance Examination to gain admission into a secondary school. I performed creditably well, placing 30th for boys and was placed at the St. Vincent Grammar School in 1980. It was a dream come true. I still remember many of my close classmates from Petersville: Brian Luke, Kerwin Horne, Dave King, Karen Drakes, Shirley Providence, Carolyn Nelson, Gaileen Hinds-Providence, Michelle Lynch, Michelle Ryan, Eardsdale Kirby and Denika Peters to name a few.

Mom's selfless love for her children and her neighbours was unmatched in the community. Her love for people was demonstrated in practical terms in the relationships she established on a day to day basis. She helped numerous unfortunate persons, she gave books, clothes, shoes and sometimes money to help the less fortunate villagers and she had blossomed into a dynamic community supporter. I think what she would be mostly remembered for is the high level of respect she exhibited for all and sundry. For example, she believed in serving the average person on the best chinaware (the very finest) and fine cutlery. Her motto was, "Treat every human being with dignity and appreciation regardless of colour, creed or class". She never believed in serving any human being, not even her pets in anything made of plastic. She believed profoundly in the power of education and farming, and had an unending passion for flowers. Mom believed that you couldn't consider yourself independent if you were not growing or rearing your own food. She was critical of most governments and policy makers of St. Vincent and the Grenadines for neglecting agriculture. I too share similar sentiments. She was very meticulous in ensuring that we spoke Standard English and at the same time she made us realize that we must have an appreciation of colloquial language. Hence she stressed that it was not dialect because the structure of the language showed that it was not broken English but a new language altogether. Dialect was a derogatory term for the language. "It is the breadfruit language that makes you Vincy to the bone," she would say, "and is what will connect you to the everyday man and vice versa".

I try to bear this in mind and execute it in my practice and was told by many of my patients that because I speak their language I am able to extract information so vital in healing them. This modus operandi is sometimes interpreted by others as being too 'grassroot' for a professional more so a doctor. These are some of the small town remnants of colonialism that still hinder the minds of many of our natives. However, I forgive my critics, because the island is still in search of its own identity. Having gained independence from Great Britain just over thirty years ago, it is trying to grapple for a place internationally as a young post colonial democracy.

I realize also that my outlook on life and my socialization with the Cuban people gave me respect, acceptance and recognition, and has set the stage for open communication with them, thus forging greater alliances which were so necessary in overcoming many of my trying circumstances while in pursuit of a medical career there.

My mother had great knowledge of the bible and used it as her guide in everyday life. She adored the book of Proverbs by King Solomon and often used it to influence our way of thinking. Mom read us these Proverbs sometimes before putting us to bed. She would always give us a kiss on the cheek before putting us to bed. I still remember that kiss as if it was yesterday, and I still see her face saying, "Goodnight, I love you, sweet dreams." It's amazing how much a parent can do for a child just by uttering these lovely words.

At home there were some things you did without question. We had household chores which we always did on weekends. We were instructed to watch and listen to the news, mom did not compromise with that. Every member of the family knew his/her specific tasks and one of mom's favourite phrases was, "Many hands make light work." She was very strict about our homework and of course washing our own socks and cleaning our shoes for the week.

Our house was a rendezvous for many of the villagers of Carriere. We were one of the few households to own a television set in the village in the late 70's, hence the whole village flocked to our house to get a glimpse of what was happening on TV, peering through the windows while some were stationary in the living room. I am sure that our home was a base for frequent interaction among villagers and I know that Carriere village is reaping the dividends from this close socialization.

Every member of my family understood that farming and animal husbandry was the heart of our existence, hence it was the duty of each member, more so my two brothers and myself to take care of the animals, namely goats, sheep, cows, pigs, rabbits, chickens and a donkey. It was the income made from the sale of these animals and the sale of produce which provided financial support to buy books, uniforms and other school supplies and to pay for transportation to and from Kingstown. At one time, we had eighty goats, sixty sheep and ten cows. Irrespective of the hour, we had to tether them on mornings before we attended school and bring them back home on evenings after school. Everyday we had our tasks cut out for us.

Psalms 136 v 1

Oh give thanks unto the Lord for he is good; for his mercy endureth forever.

Chapter 3

School days are happy, happy days

'School days are happy, happy days!' Those are the words of the calypsonian Slinger Francisco, the Mighty Sparrow. I am giving my mom most of the credit for laying the solid foundation for my educational endeavours and all my academic achievements even in the field of medicine. (Firstly to God be the Glory)

It was from inception at the Petersville Primary School that my character and personality were molded. It was in fact the hybridization of both school and home and society at large that gave me my fundamentals in civics, culture, spirituality, moral and social values. The school was holding its own in education in St. Vincent and the Grenadines and I was humbled to be part of this noble institution. My mom had made such a great decision that I would want to describe her as being a visionary in this regard, because to send us to this private school within those trying circumstances is an accomplishment worth mentioning; and it is now as an adult that I look back, I can see what she meant by 'Where there is no vision the people perish." I think we were receiving a more personal and caring education than in the public schools at that time. In the public schools there were always problems of discrepancies between teachers and government about basic facilities and amenities, teachers rights and pay and other social conditions in the late 70's and early 80's.

I don't think that mommy ever regretted sending us to the Petersville School. She was sometimes criticized by some villagers for 'playing big shot' and for sending 'country pickney to town school and private school at that'. Even some of the most affluent in the Marriaqua Valley did not make that sacrifice. Mom remained steadfast to her philosophy that the best education does not come cheap and the cheap education may not be good. That was the reality at that time. She added, "Investing in a sound education I expect to change a whole generation or two of the Toney family. The education that I am giving you will make a difference in your children and your children's children."

At the Petersville School there was a strong emphasis on discipline. The principal of the school Miss Roslyn Peters affectionately called, Miss Roslyn was a relentless disciplinarian. She made sure that grace was said four times per day. Collective prayers and hymns were sung on mornings and evenings, and on afternoons when school was dismissed. I still remember two of my favourite hymns up to today; 'Morning has Broken' and 'Now the day is Over'. Miss Roslyn kept the children on their toes while she guided her staff as a collective unit in the execution of discipline.

She carried out her task with a purpose, a vision and a mission. The school motto was, "It is only hard work that leads to success"; words that still resonate within me even at this present moment as I write this book 'The Unapologetic Quest for success". It is from those early days that my passion for knowledge, and my desire to succeed using knowledge as my vehicle for assisting the less fortunate and eradicating ignorance. It was Socrates who said, "There is only one good – knowledge and only one evil – ignorance ignited". At Petersville School, every child was responsible for maintaining the school's environs and because of this, every child assisted in keeping the school's compound clean.

I was regarded at school as one of the strongest boys. (Of course I had lots of training on the farm, lifting sacks of potatoes, eddoes and banana boxes). Many persons today still remember me as the student who opened the children's flasks for lunch. This was due to a phenomenon of expansion. When hot food was placed in the flask on mornings, it expanded and it became difficult to open and I became the one in charge of doing the honours. I still cherish these primary school memories when so many children were lining up with their flasks in hand waiting for me to perform my "duty". I can still remember these young voices, "Andy Toney, can you open this flask for me please?" It was a spectacle to behold.

I participated in numerous extra-curricular activities at the Petersville Primary School. One of my first performances on stage was with Prima Donna Bascombe, now an international recording artiste who has even appeared on MTV. We performed the song 'You Could Have

Been With me' by Sheena Easton, and at a Christmas concert held by the school 'An Old Christmas Card' by Jim Reeves. She made me dream of being a singer; I guess that was not to be, as I realized I had a few 'cockroaches in my voice.' I must confess that I have not given up completely on this dream!

The most memorable experience that I had at Petersville was about a rooster which a teacher at the school had asked me to get for her. We had none at the time and my mom had to buy one from a close neighbour Mr. 'Roggles' Constantine. The truth is, the bus conductor was told that there was a rooster inside of the bag that we had given to him and that he should be careful with it. He forgot and placed a sack of potatoes on the poor rooster, macerating it instantly. When we reached to Kingstown, we bought another bag from Doc Veira's market shop, only to discover that the fowl was dead. We disposed of it immediately in a nearby garbage bin and proceeded to school. We were a little late for school and related what had transpired to the teacher. "It's the best lie I have ever heard in my entire life," she replied. Although it was no fault of ours, up to this day I still feel guilty that this unfortunate occurrence made me lose my teacher's gift of trust in me and I could not fulfill my promise. I regret not taking the dead rooster to my teacher as evidence, it would have cleared up the whole issue.

At first, going to school in Kingstown was a bit of a culture shock. I was always amazed at how the 'town boys' had life so easy. They had little or nothing to do before or after school. I immediately began to assess both forms of life and appreciate the advantages and disadvantages of each one. I was maturing with an open mind and enjoyed every second of my primary school life. I believed that the progressive decision that my mom had taken was paying great dividends to our family. We also had a close relationship with many of our villagers and shared everything, even knowledge with our peers. Selfishness and individualism were not rampant in those days and there was community spirit among the villagers. We had great friends and neighbours like the Richardson family. We played, hunted, fished and bathed together in the rivers. In fact we played sports like Cricket, Volleyball, Rounders, Hopscotch, Dodgeball, Hide and seek (coopie) and moonlight games, I even played a game of Netball.

Some of my playmates included Levi, Judith, Francis, Elroy and Godwin Mapp, Harriette, Kenroy, Roslyn Richardson, Leonard Clarke, James

Clarke, Alfie and Sammius Clarke, Sonny and Winston McFee, Brenzil and Peter Ashton, Verrol and Beris Richardson, Homer Richardson, Garfield Joseph, Cheffy Thomas and a list too long to mention.

Both Adrian and I assisted on the farm while mom sold agricultural produce at home to traffickers who shipped them to neighbouring Caribbean islands, mainly to Trinidad and Tobago.

In those days, Trinidadians boasted that in their country money was no problem, so Vincentians flocked to Trinidad to get a share of the oil dollar. Many did so illegally and up to this day have never returned to St. Vincent. Trinidad also controlled a large percentage of the food bought from St. Vincent and the Grenadines; therefore farming was paramount to the economy. On weekends we looked forward to life in the country again, having spent almost the whole week in Kingstown.

My primary school days were climaxing, it was common entrance time and I performed creditably well placing in the first 30 boys. I had disappointed my school as everyone expected me to place in the top ten, but that was not to be. At the same time I was elated to be awarded a place at the St. Vincent Grammar School. At that time, just entering Grammar school gave you the advantage at excelling at Secondary school. From that moment onwards, I envisaged myself travelling on the road to success through knowledge along the corridors of the future and I anticipated my first day at the Grammar school.

Chapter 4

Off to the St. Vincent Grammar School. Per Aspera ad astra!

My first day at the Grammar School was one of the most interesting days of my Secondary school life. It was marked with great uncertainty and excitement. Many of the students were smartly dressed with their low cropped haircut accentuated with a part on one side of the head. We were all dressed in khaki shirts, neatly tucked into our khaki pants with cutting seams.

Each student wore his uniform with pride. The Grammar school came alive. 'Clouting', a traditional form of initiating new boys into the school was engraved in the minds of everyone who had spent a year or more at the school. I retaliated in some instances and was given extra doses by some elder students. I settled in well and started my first class. My English A and B teacher was Mr. John McLean. I still remember some of the books of English B classes; 'Tom Sawyer' and The Adventures of Huckleberry Finn. I adapted to the challenges of secondary school and at the end of the first term, I placed 1st overall for all the form 1's. For me it was an important milestone, for it meant that I had surpassed everyone who had beaten me at common entrance. It was this feat that generated in me the confidence to know deep within that I could pursue anything that I wanted passionately and succeed. The Grammar school was established about 100 years ago as the first secondary educational institution in St. Vincent and the Grenadines in colonial times. Initially the sons of poor and working class people did not enter the doors of this noble institution easily and selection for entrants was done based on different requirements. Today the Government of St. Vincent and the Grenadines has declared universal secondary education for all citizens and a place is guaranteed in the Grammar School for the student who places among the first 150 successful students at the common entrance examination.

I entered the St. Vincent Grammar School in September of 1980, one year after the island achieved independence form Great Britain. In those days, there were some philosophical linkages of the 'progressive' youth with the remnants of black power radicalism and great turbulence existed in the struggle for independence and decolonization of the Caribbean. These were the order of the day: All eyes in the village were now focused on the Carriere boy now poised to embark on an academic career at the Grammar School, and an expected trendsetter for those who would come after.

A lot was on my shoulders to perform well and also not to disappoint my village and my mom. Sometimes, an elder in the village would call me and give me advice and encouragement. I remember one elderly man always hammered these words in my head, "Keep away from bad company and people who want to belittle your ambition. Remember that small minded people will always try to belittle you, but the great ones will make you believe that one day you will be great too."

I excelled in the first year and was promoted to form 2 room 6 where all the "big guns" converged; persons like Curtis Bascombe, Cleophus George, Ian Powell, Mark Cyrus, Christopher Davy, Andrew Rogers, Dean King to name a few. We were under the keen and capable watch of Mrs. Jeanette France. I continued my academic achievement under some very trying circumstances.

In form one, our television set which had served such a valuable purpose in our home and by extension the village of Carriere ceased to work. My mom decided that she would not take it to be repaired and we did not have the privilege of seeing another television in our home again throughout my school career. To make matters worse, La Soufriere volcano had erupted in 1979 and the agricultural industry was devastated. Many crops were destroyed and there was social disruption within several communities as many persons had to be evacuated from one part of the island to another. To compound the agricultural nightmare, hurricane Allen struck in 1980 wreaking havoc on the country's economy and destroying 80% of the island's agriculture and housing. More tragedy came upon our family as this hurricane also blew off the roof of our home and destroyed almost all our belongings. Unimaginable destruction occurred in Carriere through landslides, overflowing of rivers, loss of animals and vast damage to homes and properties. The village was in distress and neighbours who weren't speaking to each other became friends once again. The village was unified in solidarity, in compassion and everyone became his brother's keeper. Through cooperation and self help, the villagers fought hard to get Carriere back on its feet.

St. Vincent's economy saw a down turn in business and all economic activity. The banks and financial institutions were reluctant to assist farmers in agricultural production and animal husbandry. The farming community, including my mom, had to take harsh measures to sustain itself to cope with these new dreadful economic and social realities. My mom was an economist and an accountant in her own right. She ingeniously and single handedly introduced various cost cutting measures in the home to balance her budget. There was no electricity in the home for over five years. That meant that I pursued my entire secondary education studying with candle light. Our family had lost thousands of dollars with the advent of these two natural disasters. Mommy knew best, we thought, and we were guided by her vision. She would say, "It's not what we have or where we are now, but where we intend to go and what we intend to gain that counts." Survival was the name of the game.

Mom had to hire workers to cultivate the farm to increase productivity. Public standpipes, natural springs and the river in our 'garden' were our best friends. There were cuts in gas, water, electricity, food and clothes to save money. Back to our roots, cooking on wood fire, coals and kerosene stove when available. In those days we ate what we grew and grew what we ate on the farm. 'Callaloo' was cut to make soup; we got the milk from the cows we reared, and eggs from the chickens. Doughboy was made with coconut and cassava, and arrowroot starch made fine porridge. Roast plantains and 'grindy' were one of my favourites accompanied by lime and passion fruit juice made from fruits picked from our trees. We drank 'bush tea' and ate dukuna, grated sweet potato boiled in banana leaves for dinner. We were never hungry. The family improvised to survive.

At Grammar School while students boasted of their ham and bacon with eggs for breakfast, I was satisfied with coconut or madongo bakes with hot chocolate with coconut milk. Sometimes on weekends we might have some crayfish, manicou with ground provision; no big deal, it was normal for us. At times it was very rough and tough; but I reiterate, we were never hungry.

My mom was the architect of this new state of affairs. She steered us out of the crisis single handedly. I have risen above formidable odds to excel at the secondary and tertiary level in my academic quest. Nevertheless, on reaching my late teens, affairs of the heart caused me to lose direction temporarily and I became distracted from school work resulting in my repeating form 4 science. Even though I had passed with 50% it was the judgment of the headmaster that I should repeat the form to have a better foundation for GCE and CXC. This was the worst experience I have ever had in my entire academic life. Everything seemed to have gone wrong. I was not my true self and school work had played second fiddle to other social activities. Music, sports and being involved in five different youth groups had drained me of all my energies. I even thought I had fallen in love at that time. Logically I didn't apply myself enough to achieve a better grade. Even though I was eligible for promotion Mr. Campbell, the then headmaster reasoned that I was still below the average age hence he proposed that I repeat form 4. I was annoyed for I believed that I had let down my teachers and my mom, but mom consoled me saying, "True greatness in a person is not measured by never falling, but by rising every time you fall." It was these words that kept me focused and they still do up to today.

I returned to form 4 Science with renewed vigour and a penchant for hard work. Repeating the class did wonders for me. I passed in the first five positions and competed with persons like, Esworth John, Colville Ferdinand, Richard Bullock, Waltz Clarke and Marcus Ballantyne to name a few. In all this turmoil and uncertainty Mrs. Andrea Keizer-Bowman was the teacher who restored my confidence at the Grammar School. I must express my sincere gratitude and appreciation to Mrs. Bowman for note worthy contribution towards my academic achievements. Mrs. Bowman was instrumental in getting me to participate in various essay competitions in 1985. I participated in the Ministry of Tourism essay contest and placed first overall. My essay topic was, 'How can Tourism be developed in St. Vincent and the Grenadines?' I structured my essay around the linkages that should be established between tourism, culture, agriculture and production. Research was done from a World Bank report on St. Vincent the previous year on how to improve and promote the tourism package for greater sustainability.

In another essay competition organized by the Ministry of Education, I placed third for the entire island. The topic was, 'World peace'. I was now maturing as a talented writer. Because of my achievements in 1985 which was declared the international year of the youth, I was selected by a panel of judges to represent St. Vincent and the Grenadines at a United Nations mock assembly held in Jamaica under the auspices of UNESCO to commemorate the "International Year of the Youth." I met persons like Bronty Wallace, Aquellah Ackbar from Antigua and Julius Gittens of Barbados. Many of the persons who attended are now prominent citizens in their respective countries.

There is an incident in Grammar School that I have battled with for years. I had scored nine out of ten in an assignment given to us by a teacher, yet I was deprived of my true grade based on the ill conceived notion that I had not done the assignment by myself. In fact she gave me six marks for my assignment subtracting three and wrote, "You did not write this work all by yourself." It was rather unfortunate and it is one of the worst grades that I have ever received for it is a grade that did not come close to what I was capable of; but today, she still remains a teacher that I respect a lot and I have forgiven her. Such actions sometimes can dampen the spirit of a potentially great student and break his confidence in himself. Why she did not believe that I was capable of such good work is beyond me.

Chapter 5

It is better to give than to receive

I inherited a sound humanitarian spirit, honour and many other positive core values from my parents. These values have been instilled in me from infancy to adulthood. I have cherished and nurtured many of the guiding principles that were taught to me and they have assisted in moulding and improving my personal life in almost every area. From experience I have come to the conclusion that in life example is the greatest teacher and that you preach what you practise and practise what you preach. In synthesis, "Actions speak louder than words". There are so many persons in this island who claim to be great citizens and they help no one unconditionally. One doesn't have to possess riches to help an underprivileged person, there are other small gestures that can touch someone's life. It was Bob Marley who once said, "If you live in this world and you haven't helped a soul, it comes as if you haven't lived." In fact, you have no legacy from which your children and grandchildren can feed. You have existed but you haven't lived.

Giving Back

Adrian my younger brother and myself saw ourselves as being a little more fortunate and privileged than many of the children of Carriere. Food was always in the home and we never went hungry. We went to school regularly. We were always well clad in our uniform with appropriate shoes and socks. Mom spent her last dollar on books, school supplies and transportation; the villagers thought we were different, special and enjoyed our company. Our home was always the centre of attraction. Both Adrian and I assisted the less fortunate children of the village with their homework, reading, mathematics, English and social studies, books and magazines, reading materials that my mom had invested in. The less academically inclined children were taken under the Toneys' fold. We tutored these students free of cost, generally on weekends. Mom at times gave our clothes to the less fortunate. It was said once that my mom took care of Carriere village. I think I have emulated my mom to some extent for my life seems to be based upon constant giving; like mother like son.

What distinguished me as an organizer and student activist during my secondary school education at the St. Vincent Grammar School was the publication of the magazine "Update", which I single handedly financed with the help of my mom. It's amazing how commitment, willingness to work, and determination to succeed can propel your ambitions and aspirations to higher heights. I had borrowed five hundred dollars from my mom to start the publication of "Update" magazine while in the Grammar School. Looking back now, my mom must have had a high level of confidence and trust in my ability as an organizer and more so my sense of responsibility within the circumstances prevailing at that time. Coliville Ferdinand my classmate was my deputy editor and Prima Donna Bascombe who attended A'level at that time was appointed secretary. The first issue of the magazine featured black inventors in history and the rise of black consciousness of the seventies along with the various movements and personalities in North America at that time. Other highlights of the magazine "Update" featured Robert Nesta Marley OM (Order of Merit) of Jamaica, entertainment news, sports and health columns. A humour page and cartoons were regular features that graced the pages of our magazine.

I was elated and satisfied with what we had produced with our limited budget. We were able to pioneer a magazine, first of its kind with a high standard of positive content. I was the chief financier and editor; in fact I held various hats to assist in the materialization of this project. As we would say here in St. Vincent, I was chief cook and bottle washer and was criticized for being a micromanager of the magazine. The highlight of my student life at the Grammar School was the success I engendered in mobilizing and unifying the secondary schools in Kingstown through 'Update'. It was labeled a masterpiece of a project that exposed the talent of various secondary school students and gave them an avenue for self expression. Many students submitted poems and articles of a social and political nature. There were also essays and a pen-pal corner. There was a page that reported on what was happening in our schools. We were able to galvanize support from the

Justice newspaper and we were granted credit to print one thousand copies. They sold like hot bread. The price was fixed at two dollars per copy and demands were greater than its supply. We actually published four issues of 'Update', we had exceeded our expectations.

Just when we thought the future looked promising, tragedy struck. I missed the supervision of an issue of the magazine and the concept of the magazine was modified to appear cool, so as to appeal to the growing audience of diverse interest. There were many requests to feature rock groups whose names I will not mention. It was a disaster, we had hit rock bottom. I was not present in St. Vincent as I had attended a two week UN mock assembly and training funded by UNESCO under the auspices of UNDP in Jamaica for I had completely missed some of the contents of the last issue of the magazine. Upon my return I was informed by some of the correspondents of the magazine that the form teacher along with the headmaster had placed a ban on the magazine. I was extremely disappointed for it was one of the reasons why I wore so many hats to guarantee that no subversive literature, especially of lewd content nor any unbalanced political views were expressed through our medium.

It was now a pet project for which I was granted the honours of reading its eulogy. Luckily, because the magazine was so profitable, we were able to pay off all the debts that we had incurred during this publication; nevertheless it was a tremendous blow.

I also was instrumental in establishing the inter-secondary school student council which came about because of the strong bonds we had formed with various students from all the secondary schools in Kingstown. I was elected assistant secretary to this prestigious student body. We had drafted our own constitution and registered our organization under the umbrella body of the National Youth Council. I still remember some of the other members who served on that student council with excellence, Karen Hinds, Leroy Dyer, Julian Farrell, Otis Joslyn and Cutbert Knights were all part of this vibrant executive. It took months of planning, meeting and painstaking hours of negotiation to achieve our objectives. The first was an incident involving two students who were expelled from school on disciplinary grounds. We intervened and had the headmaster Bertram 'Timmie' Richards reverse his decision. I remember hearing him say initially when we started the negotiation, 'I would wait until now to let school children tell me how to run my school?" We had days of discussions before Mr. Richards was persuaded to reverse his decision. That was my first real lesson in bargaining. I can remember being coached by my mom on how to achieve a better outcome with Mr. Richards. It was Julian Farrel and Rudolph Peters who did the bulk of the pleading on the students' behalf and they eventually persuaded Mr. Richards. Boy, he was a hard nut to crack.

In another case the council intervened on behalf of a Bishop's College student from Bequia. His mom lived in the United States; he didn't know his father and was renting on the mainland, his mom paying the rent to stay during the week while he would journey to Bequia on weekends. He was suspended for fighting one day and was told to bring his guardian to school. The council mediated on his behalf and the decision to suspend him was reversed and he was given a lighter punishment.

These were two very important victories of the council and it showed how a united student body can cause meaningful change and can impact on the students' lives and future. We were unitied on a single cause which was, 'the improvement of relationships between students and teachers.' I am sure that we had transformed the way teachers looked at students and vice versa. One thing I'd learnt though, is that although we live in democracy, the way we conduct business is unreflective of this system of government, especially in the running of organizations and institutions.

Carriere you are always on my mind

It was my desire to give back something to the community that moulded and propelled me. It was because of this that I organized the first broad based community organization during the early 1980's. We organized many educational programmes including lectures, seminars, symposiums and other cultural presentations. One of our resource personnel was an American, Richard Pelligrino who conducted an ongoing programme on substance abuse. Mr. Pelligrino had vast experience in this field as he was an ex-drug addict. His expertise and experience went a long way in ensuring that there were meaningful and interesting discussions on the subject of drugs and drug abuse. We invited other groups from the Marriaqua Valley to participate in these discussions. The lectures were always well received by the groups and the community at large. In addition, Mr. Pelligrino had asked me to write a chapter in a book that he had conceptualized. I wrote a piece on what developed countries needed to know about poorer countries before disbursing funds for assistance. (I don't know if this book was ever published)

Hilltop blossomed into a vibrant community based group and we were very active in sports. Our organization participated in many national sporting competitions. We fielded teams in soccer, drafts, cricket, netball, dominoes, volleyball, table tennis and athletics. The Hilltop teams did well in Marriaqua competitions and held our own in national sporting events. On behalf of Hilltop I was able to contact Wilfred Slack, a Vincentian who played for Middlesex and England cricket teams. (May God bless his soul.) Mr. Slack assisted the team in securing cricket gear and other assistance.

We were also engaged in several environmental projects in Carriere. Such projects included planting and cutting hedges, planting trees to beautify the community and the upkeep of the Carriere Cemetery. We did our fair share of community work. However, all was not work. We also organized parties; Goat cooks and beach splashes. We interacted well with the rest of the community. We were able to stage the first curry night ever in St. Vincent and the Grenadines in 1984, it was a great success. We had organized this as a fun venture to purchase sporting gear for various sporting activities.

Carriere was bustling with persons. There was traffic jam and there were many vehicles in the village that night. Persons from all walks of life came to sample the curry night. We had prepared curried mutton, curried beef, curried pork, curried fish, curried conch, curried manicou and iguana and also roti. We also had many other dishes like curried peas and beans. Our club had never catered for so many persons at one time. We had prepared for two hundred and fifty persons, but had to replenish our stocks and cater for an additional two hundred and fifty persons. Glen Jackson had done a wonderful job in promoting our activity (may God Bless his soul) and the theme song was Hurry, Hurry come for Curry by Geane Scaramuzzo of Trinidad. The music was fabulous; DJ Alexander the Great provided the music while Al Trotman was the MC and toastmaster. From the proceeds raised from the curry night we were able to assist in the purchasing of books, uniforms, and school supplies for persons whom we had sponsored from the community. Mom used to say St. Vincent and the Grenadines would become a better place if the 'haves' shared a little more with the 'have nots'. And then she would admit, "But on the other hand, how do we think the 'haves' got their riches? Of course it's by not sharing with the 'have nots'."

I still aspire one day to sponsor at least fifty students to attend secondary school and fifty to primary school, students from the most under-privileged backgrounds in society. This is one of the ways I hope to make a difference to the island that I love and cherish so much, keeping steadfast to the national pledge "Land of my birth I pledge to thee, my loyalty and devotion, in all I think and say and do" and also the first verse of the national anthem, of Saint Vincent and the Grenadines

"Saint Vincent! Land so beautiful,

With joyful hearts we pledge to thee

Our loyalty and love, and vow

To keep you ever free."

You see, you can't say the national pledge and national anthem without thinking of educating the children who are less fortunate. Maybe it's because of my early socialization in Cuba where secondary education is compulsory and tertiary education is accessible, once you have the desire and not necessarily the money. Therefore, financial and educational sources will have to be sourced. Writing this book is the beginning of the Lucy Toney foundation to support all these charities. I'm sure mom would be quite pleased with our efforts.

Chapter 6

Volunteerism without boundaries

My voluntary work was not confined only to St. Vincent and the Grenadines. In Cuba volunteerism is institutionalized. It is the civic duty of each Cuban to perform voluntary services under the constitution of Cuba, more so promotion to any post is not only based on academic skills or job performance, it is rooted also in how many hours of voluntary service you would have performed.

I participated in Camagüery province where students traditionally performed Cuartelero duties. This was really one day of voluntary work where each student was his brother's keeper on the campus. We took time out to clean the dormitory and general surroundings. It was a positive initiative and was aimed at humbling you. I recall the son of an African president who had studied in England, then ended up in Cuba to pursue a career in medicine. He was outraged at the thought of a task that was gruelling both psychologically and physically. He was told by the dean that he was not in England or his parents' palace and that this was the way they did the business of educating in Cuba. "We do not look down upon any type of work here." My African friend buckled up and attempted the task. (He surely came around!) Then there was 'trabajo voluntario' in which the University students were involved in voluntary work within the community and agricultural farms during a fifteen day period, generally at the end of the academic year. We lived, worked, ate, slept and had recreational activities on the farm site. For the foreign students it was an optional programme. However, I enjoyed the socialization quite well after having worked on our own farm at home. I periodically spent half my vacations on the farm. This was a very enjoyable experience and I learnt a lot about Cuba's agricultural practices.

I learnt about the soil types existing there and also about the soil chemistry and how to test the soil to adapt agricultural practices to replenish the minerals in the soil before and after harvesting. I also learnt about biological pesticides in certain crops.

No task was too dirty or degrading for all of the young aspiring doctors to perform. Then we were in winners' row. Our brigade was adjudged the most disciplined and organized in all of the medical science faculties in Cuba. We were given a house on the beach in Guanabacoa for one weekend with all expenses paid by the Cuban Government. We were responsible for unloading twenty trucks each with a trailer of potatoes grown in Guines and packing them into a refrigerated warehouse for distribution to other state outlets. The warehouse was gigantic and the cold storage temperature was almost freezing point. We worked hard and were able to accomplish the task. I was the only foreign student who took part in this grueling work.

I also performed voluntary service in the medical field during my post-graduate studies in Cuba. The knowledge and valuable skills became quite useful in supervising Earl 'Ole George' Daniel and Joel Butcher in breaking the world record in endurance walking, though not recognized by the Guinness Book of World Records. I believe that I was fortunate to have worked along with members of Cuba's sports academy, sports medicine and Cuban physiotherapists. I have gained a wealth of knowledge which I was able to use in breaking the world record in endurance walking four times through Earl 'Ole George' Daniel and Joel Butcher. Three cheers we did it and that cannot be disputed.

Cuban trainers are very meticulous in the preparation of their sportsmen and women. The trainers work assiduously on the mental toughness of the athletes, no wonder their records regionally and internationally speak for themselves. The West Indies Cricket team and board need to take a page out of their book.

I continue to give back to my island medically in tangible ways. I am a visiting doctor with the Rotary Club International here in St. Vincent through their health programme, 'The Village Doctor'. This is an ongoing medical assistance programme for underprivileged areas in St. Vincent and the Grenadines. It is through this programme that I came face to face with the unfair severity of health problems and the socio-economic and political impact of poverty on our people.

My most memorable visit to date was at Langley Park in 2003, a rural village of Georgetown, 22 miles from capital Kingstown. I attended the clinic as an Obstetrician/Gynaecologist, but that memorable day I was a real general practitioner, attending to cases of every imaginable specialty in medicine. It was an exceptional experience. I was shocked to see the challenging conditions of these rural folk, and the appalling environment and degradation of the village. It really touched me and I gave my best working overtime. I medically attended eighty or so patients while another eighty or more were awaiting medical assistance late into the night. There were about six other doctors and a normal village doctor visit; we all attended twenty persons on average. Eighty persons must have been a rotary club record for one physician. I read about some of these conditions that I saw only in my medical textbooks.

I could only remember reading and having my professor showing us photos of children in such horrific conditions existing in poor under developed countries, but I could not imagine that in my own homeland these medical conditions were evident. Though not common, they exist. No wonder the Prime Minister Dr. Ralph Gonsalves has earmarked this area for the establishment of a modern diagnostic centre being built by the Cuban government. This centre is urgently needed. This will enable the people of Langley Park and by extension the people of St. Vincent and the Grenadines to access state of the art medical attention in this fierce competitive global economy, threatened by economic meltdown and unequal trade between developed and underdeveloped countries.

Chapter 7

Charity begins at home

During my nine years of work and service in St. Vincent and the Grenadines as a medical doctor, I came across numerous problems faced by friends, family members and disadvantaged persons.

I was completing my post graduate degree, I had just finished my final exams at Calixto Garcia Hospital. I stood before a panel of distinguished judges made up of eminent Obstetrician/Gynaecologist in Cuba-Professor Ramon Butaka, Professor Antonio Gomez and Professor Taica Roque. Professor Antonio Gomez said, "You have performed well in your exams and as from now you are given the title of Obstetrician/Gynaecologists. However I am cautioning you that your greatest characteristic in being a doctor should be your humanity. I would be disappointed in you if one day I should hear that you are exploiting the poor while working in your country. I wouldn't be happy to know that I was responsible in part for such a heartless human being, who parades as a doctor. Cuba may be a poor country, but in medicine I believe we are one of the most humane countries on earth in taking care of our citizens. You have lived here, you have worked here, and I hope that some aspect of this humanity would have rubbed off on you and that you will take it to your country. We do not profess to have a perfect country, but one thing about Cuba is that, we strive for a humane system of medicine."

In all my years in Cuba if there is one thing that still boggles my mind is the fact that such a poor country can provide free medical attention to its citizens, and it is because of the words of persons like professor Antonio Gomez that I have continued to sponsor under-privileged children to school and assist many unfortunate citizens of this blessed island St. Vincent and the Grenadines.

Internationalist Activities in Grenada

Returning from New York in mid September 2004 I saw some of the horrific images of Grenada after the passage of hurricane Ivan. I was saddened by this hurricane ravished island. It was like nothing I had seen before. The Rotary Club contacted me to accompany them to Grenada as a visiting Obstetrician/Gynaecologist to assist the Grenadian people. Then it dawned on me that this could be my contribution to the Grenadian people in their hour of need.

The club, a multidisciplinary team of about 200 persons, including construction workers, doctors, pharmacists, dentists to name a few, departed Port Kingstown on October 2004 for Grenada by boat with approximately half a million dollars worth of items. I enjoyed the boat ride to Grenada. Upon reaching there, the reality became even more shocking than in the photos I had seen. The island looked like a virtual battlefield; buildings were completely destroyed. It was as though an atomic bomb was dropped on the island; Hiroshima and Nagasaki came to mind. The havoc caused by hurricane Ivan seemed too much for such a small island.

The division of religion, class or race meant nothing at that time, for the basic human aspiration was survival. Food had to be rationed in the shelters and money meant very little as there was nothing to buy. I struggled to contain my emotions, then I heard pharmacist Matthew Thomas saying, "Don't worry, Grenadians are a resilient people and they will rebuild their country soon." I felt relieved on hearing such inspiring words and optimism. Today Grenada has proven Matthew Thomas right.

We worked along with some of our Grenadian counterparts, some of whom I still keep in contact with. The experience was fascinating and I prayed to the Lord that St. Vincent and the Grenadines does not experience such a catastrophe anytime in the future. Grenada made me understand that the manmade divisions of society mean so little in such circumstances. I returned with graphic images of tarpaulin over the roofs of houses embedded in my memory. I remained pensive for a long time reflecting on how the building codes in St. Vincent and the Grenadines should be standardized and regulated by competent authorities to withstand the wrath of such hurricanes, and I couldn't help pondering on the words of Che Gueverra, "The life of a single human being is worth much more than all the wealth of the world's richest men put together."

Chapter 8

From Hairoun to Havana

I remember that day when I was offered a medical scholarship to study in Havana. It was the end of July 1987. I was not having a particularly good day, but on learning that a scholarship from Cuba was offered for Vincentians to study medicine, I began to feel very optimistic and very positive within myself and all my mom's advice seemed to have been rushing in my brain at once. Reach for the stars, think positive, the sky is your limit don't let anyone distract you from your goals, reach for your goals without violating moral codes and common sense.

I reminisced on how the Lord had been so good to me. Here I was trying to finish A'levels to get the requisite subjects and grades to pursue medicine and all this was erased in the wink of an eye. Mom would say, what doesn't happen in a thousand years, happens in a second. The message came to me via Dalton Preddie and though I was excited I was in a state of denial. I had gotten an epiphany sometime in the past where I was given the scholarship above everyone who had applied and at that moment I knew the hour had arrived. It had been four years since the last scholarship was given to the UPM by the Cuban Government, and from then I had remained cautiously optimistic of my selection. I was advised by Dalton Preddie to go to Kingstown forthwith for there were others who would be vying for the scholarship, as I needed to be interviewed at the party's office. I began bracing myself for the unexpected.

Immediately, I told my mom. She was somewhat excited but listened attentively. She never objected to my pursuit of an education and I didn't have to tell her much to persuade her about my studying in Cuba, at least that's what I thought. To my surprise I was confronted with some serious questions, some of which I had no answers for. "I want you to become a doctor as you desire, but not in Cuba. I have never prepared my mind for this." Then I looked at her smiling and replied, "You see mom, scholarships for medicine are rarely given by any other country. It is only Cuba who gives these scholarships to thousands of poor people's children from all over the world and this is the best opportunity for me. I can't wait for tomorrow, for tomorrow no one has seen."

She looked out of the window peering into the sky and said in a low tone, "Andy, I hear so much negative things about Cuba and life over there that I'm concerned. Castro is not an easy man, he is a dictator, I don't feel comfortable. I wouldn't want anything to happen to you, you know what I mean." I listened without replying. She paused in quiet reflection as though my decision was the right one in the present circumstances. Her eyes, moved from left to right as I waited anxiously for a positive response.

She smiled and put her hands on my shoulder and said, "My faith in the Lord has always served me well. With God's blessing and spiritual guidance you will succeed." She emphatically agreed that I should take the scholarship and I had to remind her that it wasn't given to me yet. "When I was younger I wanted to be a doctor," she added, "but my ambitions were interrupted by the decision to start a family." The closest I came to being a doctor was working as a dental nurse with Dentist Payne. I learnt quickly and in no time Dr. Payne was leaving the clinic in my care while he took prolonged holidays to Europe. I performed most of the procedures that a dentist would have done in a clinic, from extractions, fillings, cyst removal and even the making of dentures. You see I couldn't become a doctor and God fulfilled my dreams through you." I reminded her that I had not gotten the scholarship yet, but she replied that this was already taken care of from above.

I kissed mom goodbye and set off to prepare myself for the interview. I had tried to look as formal as possible as mom always said, "You don't get a second chance to make a first impression." She gave me money for transportation, photocopying of my certificates and some pocket change. I felt adrenaline rushing into my body then suddenly I felt nervous about the pace at which everything was unfolding. It was the longest ride ever for me from Carriere to Kingstown. My mind was uncontrollably darting from one subject to another and I began to reflect on the dramatic turn of events. I couldn't believe that this renewed hope was passing my way; it was as though I was in a movie.

Surprisingly the interview was very simple and down to earth. I was comfortable and felt very relaxed. I began answering questions about my academic achievements and social activities. The small panel was surprised to know that I was an executive member of four different groups at the same time. I was quite familiar with everyone on the panel which was composed of Mr. Oscar Allen, Adrian Saunders (now justice Saunders) and Arthur Bobb. They all alluded to the most important criteria for the scholarship. Upon completion of my studies, I should return home to work in St. Vincent and the Grenadines. Arthur Bobb declared, "There are no strings attached, no bonds to be signed, no fees to be paid directly to the party." He continued, 'Unfortunately the party does not offer any monetary assistance so your family will have to assist you. The party will take care of any administrative cost of getting you to Cuba. The Cuban government will pay for the ticket to travel to Cuba and when you are finished they will also pay the cost of returning you home."

There were some financial challenges which I had to overcome. I had to raise funds to facilitate some of the expenses in travelling to Cuba. Time was running out and I had only a few weeks to prepare. Mom sold a cow and our headache had ended. We were able to raise money to buy new clothes and food items as I was told that food was a scarcity in Cuba. One past student informed me, "Cuba is a country where everything is scarce so carry everything and anything."

I was now set to pursue a medical career in one of the strangest countries on earth. I had two hundred US dollars as my budget to pursue a seven year medical scholarship. I took the first step of all the steps to change my life forever. I left St. Vincent on 17th September 1987 in the midst of a tropical depression. I view this as a symbolic moment and not a superstitious one. In my travelling bag I had a copy of the Holy Bible and a collection of Caribbean Poems from Cuba to Guyana, photographs of my family and close friends and a little bottle of alcolado Glacial, shilling oil, a package of mauby bark, posters of St. Vincent and the Grenadines, a collection of calypsos from 1987 carnival, my Michael Jackson Jacket and a large flag of St. Vincent and the Grenadines. All these possessions I held dear to my heart throughout my studies in Cuba.

I boarded the plane at the then Arnos Vale Airport after saying goodbye to my family. Little did I know it would have been the last time in six years I would have had the opportunity to be with them physically. As the plane took off I said goodbye to the land that I had grown to love and cherish with all my heart, and I would spend the rest of my eleven years promoting and defending. The words of Alston 'Beckett' Cyrus reverberated in my head as the island receded from my sight.

"St. Vincent my homeland, you gave me no mansion,

No gold no diamond yet I love you a million.....

chorus

I love you St. Vincent

Sweet little island St. Vincent

...................................".

Chapter 9

University Life

My first day at medical school was just as vivid as my first day at the Grammar school. I woke up early that morning at 4:00 and could not go back to sleep. I was elated, anxious and nervous at the same time. This was certainly a dream come true. I was finally entering the doors of a medical school, which to me symbolized the first step of a long journey.

I spent one year in Camagüey studying Spanish and other preparatory classes for medical school. We also studied the history of Cuba which I somehow rejected but excelled at due to the fact that I wanted no hindrance in pursuit of a medical career. I recall arguing with my professor Emily Sanchez and questioning her. "Why do we have to do the history of Cuba? I came here to study medicine, not to be a historian." Professor Sanchez looked at me and said, "Chester, history is about a people's past, their present accomplishments and their struggles to prevent mistakes in their past being repeated in the future. This helps you to remain focused and cherish what you have achieved through blood, sweat and tears. I had heard this same statement while in St. Vincent, but in Cuba's context it had hit home and I began to understand the history of Cuba and of my own country. She continued, "We are not trying to make a simple doctor out of you, we are trying to make a revolutionary doctor, a doctor capable of transforming his immediate realities with a concise knowledge of history." I kept remembering these precious words of Professor Sanchez while I was preparing for my mission to become a medical doctor.

I reflected on my own realities in St. Vincent and took a deep breath and said to myself this first step is a big step forward for my family. Once I succeed I would have blazed a trail for other members of my family to follow.

Setting foot in a University was an accomplishment for my family and my village by extension. After all, only scholars attended university; this I was told by a teacher at the Grammar school. I contemplated whether or not I would be able to finish my medical career. I had heard so many stories about persons who had a nervous breakdown while studying medicine. While in the classroom, I said a prayer, "Father God, I know you brought me here to this strange country because you wanted me here. I know you will not depart from me. I trust your guidance and I don't believe you would have brought me this far to fail. I trust in you and I know you will open my mind and protect me from my enemies. These mercies I ask in your son Jesus Christ's name." And I was ready, come what may.

Most of the students in my class were from strong medical backgrounds, many of them had family members or other relatives who were very prominent in Cuba's leading Universities and hospitals. I felt somewhat intimidated but at no time inferior as one of my mom's favourite quotations kept revolving in my mind. 'Above you there is no one, only God, his son Jesus Christ and the skies; below you is the earth and we are all living until we all go beneath it.'

Coming from a small island state I was beginning to feel threatened by some of the students from some of the larger countries such as Spain and Greece. I remembered a student from India, Sunil making fun of me, saying that all of the people in my country could hold in their Eden Fardens Stadium in the city of Calcutta in India. Later, we became very close friends. He was captain of the 'Rest of the world' cricket team at the University while I was vice captain of the 'West Indies' cricket team at soft ball cricket. It was the first time the majority of Cubans were ever seeing the game of cricket played. Before I left St. Vincent to travel to Cuba, Julian Farrell one of the founding members of the inter-secondary school student council had advised me on hearing about my plans to study in Cuba. "Boy try not to go crazy over there Ches, medicine is no joke career.' Those words kept ringing in my head and I fought tirelessly and courageously to be disciplined and focused. I was cognizant from day one of the need to balance academics with recreation, rest and social activities to triumph in the end, which most of all meant keeping my mental stability by any legitimate means necessary.

I was fortunate, but mom would say, 'blessed' while others would say 'lucky', to overcome some of the trying circumstances of this "special period" in Cuba. I reminisce now on some of the hardships, food scarcity, transportation difficulties, and lack of basic necessities on a daily basis. Some students who could not come to grips with these harsh realities decided to return home while others were recalled by their governments. It was rough, really rough.

Speaking about rough, there was a student from Jamaica who incidentally ended up with the alias 'Rough' sticking to him. He had called home and was speaking to his mom from a phone booth. We were hearing his conversation loudly coming from the international phone booth, "Mommy the place rough, the bus system rough, mommy the food rough, the weather rough, life on campus rough, it real rough."

Everyone was asked to do some belt tightening during the 1990's in Cuba. No one starved though for lack of food. We were given a top class education but we had to make sacrifices. We had to be creative, innovative and become proficient in the art of budgeting, separating your needs from your wants. We experienced power outages and no electricity at the campus for hours.

However, students bought battery operated lights or other types of lamps. If you were not so fortunate, you went to the hospital or clinic library. Water was sometimes a problem for the first two years of my career. We woke up at 5a.m. to fill drums or containers of water. The ration lines grew longer and there were always long lines wherever you went. The crime levels were soaring. There was a student from Angola who was robbed and almost killed for a Russian made bicycle while the son of a famous meteorologist was robbed and killed allegedly for a BMX bicycle. I had my fair share of the robbers too. I was robbed one night in a bus stop in Playa and my Citizens watch was taken. It was a nightmare. Luckily my knowledge and training in Judo saved my life after wrestling and defeating him. However my watch fell off my hand and the robber escaped with one of my dearest possessions.

Failure was definitely out of my books, I could not let down my family, my country and the UPM who had provided me with this golden opportunity. I braced myself for the long haul and decided whatever the circumstances may be, I was returning home alive by the grace of God and also with the accolades of Obstetrician/Gynaecologist behind my name. Failure was not an option and success through knowledge was my only goal as I was not taking my eyes off the target.

Today I still remember more than anytime in Cuba, my first lesson in medical school. Professor Humberto, professor of anatomy at Giron preclinical and basic sciences institute wrote two words upon the overhead projector. To cut a long story short, they were 'necrophagia' and 'necrophilia'. Then he asked if we knew the meaning of these two words. You can imagine in an amphitheatre of about two hundred students about four persons showed their hands to answer including me. I was the only foreigner with my hand raised and he asked me directly to respond and I responded "Necrophilia is an abnormal love for dead bodies. Necrophagia is the act or practice of eating a corpse or carrion. This I had learnt in my first year at A'level while in St. Vincent. The students were stunned, many were asking where I had leant that. Professor Humberto congratulated me and up to today I still consider that question to be one of the most important questions in my medical career, for it meant that I saw myself on par with the best there was. From that day onwards, I was highly respected and I tried hard to live up to their expectations. It was just as mom said, "You don't get a second chance to make a first impression." From that day onwards I knew I had the ability to compete with the best there was at that time. Kwame Nkrumah's words lingered in my brain, 'A secret of success in life is to have no fear.'

Having no fear was how I confronted the first lessons of Marxism/ Leninism. I eagerly looked forward to the high level of political debate that the subject generated in class. I was labeled as having ideological problems according to my Marxism teacher as I never saw eye to eye with him, given the fact that I came from a different political system. Though I did not agree with a lot that was being taught in the philosophy classes, the classes held my attention and they were just as important as any other subject on the school's curriculum. The professor one day said to me, "Chester I know you have some problems in accepting teachings of political philosophy and scientific socialism and I understand you, but you cannot have an ideology unless you have a philosophical view of life." And he vociferously emphasized the point that philosophy shapes your mind and consequently your behaviour and stimulates your thoughts in a positive or negative way.

Looking back I think he was right and as I matured I realized how Cuba's philosophical view of medicine as a right of all and not the privilege of a few had eventually shaped my own way of seeing medicine in general. Although my professor and I did not see eye to eye mostly because of my spiritual background, I tried to understand as much as I could. After classes I went to the library to research philosophy and all the other subjects extensively. But I must confess philosophy gave me a run for my money. I eventually became highly proficient in the subject and overcame any fear that I had in the beginning, but it was not smooth sailing though.

Cuba 1990-1998

There were numerous challenges coping with the day to day life in Cuba. I had to make great changes in my personal life style, some very drastic. I had to change my eating habits and general way of living. I often ate rice, beans and eggs during most of my years in Cuba, that is up to my graduation in 1994. I learnt to drink yogurt as there was an abundance for breakfast, lunch and dinner. We had the privilege of taking one litre of yogurt after each meal. I too became accustomed to this. There were the days when we had some rest from the three musketeers (rice, beans and eggs) and chicken, beef, pork or some other variable was served. Household appliances comparatively speaking were hard to come by at the local stores. However, before the 'special period' in 1990, I observed that the Cubans owned their own washing machine, blender, coffee percolator, electric kettle, rice cooker and pressure cooker, most of these items from the Soviet Union. This I noted because many homes in St. Vincent at that time did not have all these amenities as yet. I also noted that before 1990 every Cuban bought a leg ham for their entire family while in St. Vincent a leg of ham was expensive and was only eaten at Christmas time. I started to compare and contrast Cuba to St. Vincent in the early 80's up to 1990, and I realized at that point why the revolution had succeeded for so long. I recalled in the 'pre-peristroika' period, Cubans bought a tub of ice cream every weekend and shared with family and friends. I found it quite strange for we ate ice cream for birthdays and special occasions. The most shocking aspect of my comparison was the extent to which internal tourism was practised. Every Cuban eagerly anticipated spending his or her vacation at a hotel each year either by hard work or by stimulus packages that the government gave to its best workers. Opportunity to travel overseas was limited because of the government's policy.

There were often benefits that the Cubans enjoyed, unheard of in developed and developing western countries, benefits such as free education for its citizens from the cradle to the grave. This is to say education is obligatory, that's why Cuba can boast of that famous statistic of being one of the most literate countries on earth.

In the area of medicine, Cuba offers free medical attention to all its citizens. You can have a heart or kidney transplant free of cost. There are also opportunities for its citizens to excel in sports, music, culture and the arts in general. It is like the Cubans say, 'We don't have a perfect society but we have a humane delivery of the social services.'

I have always marveled at the way Cuba has been able to keep up with the rest of the world in medicine. For example, I paid fifty pesos (equivalent to 1US dollar at that time) for most of my books. Cuba is able to translate the best books from anywhere in the world and make them available to their students.

Cuban Food

There are a number of foods that I had to get accustomed to very quickly in order to survive the hard times. For example I ate Rana (also called mountain chicken in Dominica) barbequed pork, turtle and once, alligator meat. Survival was the name of the game and I was not 'bringing last'. I liked a fruit in Cuba called Mamay. It makes a very tasty and refreshing juice.

Looking back on my life in Cuba, I must say I miss the Malécon a great deal. The Malécon is the equivalent of a sea wall with a massive wall and the sea splashing against the backdrop of an open ocean. On the Malécon we bought all varieties of food ranging from fruits to Cuban dishes. It is a place where you can buy almost anything. There was a time in 1988 that I had not eaten for almost a day, for I was still suffering from a bit of culture shock. I was starving, not because I didn't have any food, but because I wasn't accustomed to the taste of the Cuban food as yet. It was overbearing and I was invited to the home of Pedro, a good friend. Pedro was from a province in the interior called Camagüey. Pedro said to me, "We have horse meat in onion sauce." I was a bit surprised, I had never eaten horse meat in my life, but I was too hungry to say no; wow it was tasty! I had horse meat in onion sauce with rice and stewed beans with sautéed vegetables and lemonade. The Cubans have a belief that when you are anemic, horse meat is one of the fastest hemoglobin building foods that you can eat. They would tell you quite frankly, if you are anemic, eat horse meat and spinach with okra. This I have proven on many occasions where I had to postpone a surgical operation. And after advising the patient to eat the above mentioned food, within one week their hemoglobin would be surprisingly normal.

Cuba had a great diversity of delicious food. I will refrain from going into any detailed explanation about any of these foods. All I can say, if you ever go to Cuba, tasting is believing.

Cuban Culture exposed

I took my first photographs in Cuba with Don Quixote Statue in Vedado. These photographs are my mental images up to this day of my encounter with Cuban Culture. I liked to walk the Pomenard of Obispo Street in Old Havana. It was common to see that even in the hardship that the people were experiencing there were many couples walking hand in hand, sometimes kissing, having a romantic evening. One could never tell from just watching these people that there was an economic blockade for over forty years at that time placed on Cuba. The expression of the people did not reflect this reality. I too still have my own romantic memories in Paseo in Vedado and Empedrado in Old Havana.

I was pleasantly surprised at the diversity, versatility and passion of the Cubans, for anyone going to Cuba for the first time will be amazed and excited to witness the artisans who openly display such high quality craft in the streets of Havana daily. Painters, Artists, Poets, Musicians, Magicians, Ventriloquists, Jugglers; Old Havana is truly the melting pot of artistry in Cuba. To see how all these persons compete at the same time for the attention of the busy public is a spectacle to behold.

Tropicana nightclub is where the movers and shakers of Cuban society meet and greet each other. It is an exceptional place for a fantastic night out. The mood is ecstatic, the ambience, set designs, lightings, choreography are all mind boggling. It's an experience of a lifetime. At Tropicana nightclub you would experience why Cuba was dubbed the Paris of the West.

Post Graduate Studies

Completing my post graduate training in Obstetrics and Gynaecology posed severe challenges to me personally and by extension my immediate family. I did not have the support of the government at home or of any other organization. I had borrowed monies from the National Commercial Bank to finance a part of my tuition fees. Lacking funds to take care of my other expenses was nerve wracking. Mom said to me, "Andy just start your studies and leave the rest to me, and in the end the Lord will see you through." And in the end He really did see me through.

At times I felt like giving up, there were times when I questioned myself on whether I had made the right decision to specialize in Cuba. Many of the students felt that I was overly ambitious, crazy or simply stupid. They often remarked, 'Chester go home and work, experience how it feels to work for some valuable currency, drive a big jeep, wear some good clothes, eat in a posh restaurant, enjoy life from the eyes of a doctor. You are here paying the Cubans to study and work while they are not paying you one cent. You are paying the government twice, I thought you were more intelligent than that." I have learnt a meaningful lesson from some of these detractors, for one of the same persons who tried to discourage me later returned to Cuba, self-financing his own specialty at an even higher price for tuition.

Luckily I remembered the words of King David and I still use them as a guide in my everyday life, 'for all is vanity and vexation of the spirit.' I often contemplate on some of the friends who had supported me through these very rough years. I remembered Dr. Mario Calzadillo Cruz of Camagüey who practically fathered me in the initial years in Camagüey. Mario is a top class Cuban surgeon from Camagüey with specialized training and experience in organ transplant. He also worked in Guyana and Ethiopia in the early 80's and led the Cuban Medical Mission to South Africa after Nelson Mandela became president. His mother and father who I call Madre and Padre took care of me just like their own son while I was in Camagüey. Thank you Madre and Padre and I hope Madre you recover from your extensive surgery.

Another family who helped me was the Menendez family of Vedado. Nilda, Niurka and her mom America were able to help me after I had experienced one of the worst days of my life having no roof over my head. From then I do believe in the saying, that the night gets darkest just before it dawns. This was so applicable with the Menendez family. With help from my family at home and my close Cuban friends and family, I was obligated to succeed; I became a wizard in financial planning and management again. I learnt to appreciate the value of money and more importantly friendship.

Pursuing post-graduate studies as a self financed resident, I had limited funds which could not take care of my housing and other expenditure. I sought accommodation with families off campus and it was because of this that my image of Cuba changed drastically. I was now living with ordinary Cubans and interacting with everyone.

The first house where I rented was filled with persons both day and night. Everyone came for some form of medical attention for all sorts of ailments. I treated pregnant women, cancer patients, women with 'illegal professions', and a range of medical problems. They were treated with both alternative and conventional medicine. They appreciated my service and sometimes brought me rice, sugar, beans, fruits and vegetables as gifts at times as a gesture to show their profound appreciation of my humane services. Many of the ladies in the 'illegal profession' bought me shirts, pens and sometimes even watches, and shoes; they really made my day. At times while attending in my home clinic, I felt guilty and asked myself, 'Am I committing a crime against the state? Can I be arrested and charged with a felony?' The question was transferred by an incident involving a fugitive who while escaping from the police had hurt his back jumping over a wall and was unable to walk. He was brought to my home clinic and his two colleagues demanded that I assist him. I proceeded to do chiropractic adjustments to his back. This I had learnt out of medical school. He was in excruciating pain and had a luxation of the right shoulder with a sub-luxation of the Atlas Vertebra. This provoked a Brachial Plexus Neuritis. He also suffered from a luxation of the pelvis. Conventionally, because of the pain that he was experiencing, these adjustments would be done under anesthetics. But he could not go to the hospital as he was a fugitive. After the adjustment I gave him tablets of Piroxican, a tablet produced in Cuba which is used for moderate and severe pain. He felt better within fifteen minutes. His colleagues thanked me and left. I had seen his colleagues on other occasions and they told me that he was doing just fine, he couldn't be better.

This was my calling, I pondered. I had to help the sick regardless of who they were. I have always wondered whether I could have been charged for aiding and abetting a fugitive. One of his colleagues bought me a leg of ham to express his gratitude one month later. I still wonder if my patient was ever caught by the police. I never knew for what reason he became a fugitive and if he was ever caught.

There is an experience in my post-graduate studies that is still a marvel to me. As I was physically fit, I rode a bicycle about 20 miles to go to work. I lived at San Miguel de Padrón Reparto Monterrey to be exact and I rode from there to Fajardo hospital to do a rotation in general surgery. I rode with another surgeon, Professor Roberto Flachas by my side. He was the chief surgeon of the intensive care unit at Fajardo Hospital. I was very fit physically then. Bicycles became a necessity as a main source of transportation. Cuba manufactured hundreds of thousands of bicycles while China and Russia sold them also to deal with the fuel crisis. It was very practical to use a bicycle to commute instead of walking or waiting several hours for a bus, which was normal during the crisis of 'special period'.

All was not about studies for me while in Cuba. I participated in some live theatre drama and performed in many plays like Julius Caesar in the famous Shakespearean masterpiece. One of the most famous speeches that I delivered in Cuba was at the Caribbean House in Mariañao to celebrate Caribbean day. I had to address an audience of about a thousand persons including students. The speech was well received and I was given a standing ovation. I thanked the students for giving me the opportunity to represent their interests and to be able to assist in selling St. Vincent and the Grenadines and its history. What stood out in the memory of the students was the surprisingly short period of slavery that existed in St. Vincent and the Grenadines, which was just under forty years. I also highlighted that West African traders visited St. Vincent formerly called Yurumein before Columbus came. I spent some time outlining to the attentive audience the heroic epic battles fought by our National hero and Paramount Chief Joseph Chatoyer in the garifuna battles with the British invaders of our land. They were spellbound to hear our rich history. Joseph Chatoyer's life was also featured in one of the early Broadway films which highlighted his life and battles.

In concluding this chapter I would like to say that I still adhere to the advice of Fidel Castro who said, "I am not training you to be a doctor but a revolutionary doctor who sees poverty, sickness and the unequal interchange of resources and services as your prime enemies." I've kept these lofty ideas in my mind and will continue to support charities, the needy in my country and abroad on a consistent basis. Let's consider this, if you have a million dollars and you give a thousand to charity, that's really nothing in comparison to someone who has twenty dollars and gives ten for a worthy cause or someone who gives of his time to a worthy cause.

Chapter 10

New Medicine

As a young and enthusiastic Obstetrician/Gynaecologist fresh out of medical school with a passion to make a contribution to the development of the land of my birth, I was stopped in my tracks. From that day up to today I understand what it means that a prophet has no honour in his homeland.

I had my first encounter with the status quo who began to belittle my accomplishments, ridicule my achievements, ultimately marginalizing me. "He is no doctor," they scoffed, "He is a bush doctor," alluding to the fact that I had a postgraduate diploma in alternative medicine. There were all sorts of comments to question my credentials. One high ranking official in the Ministry of Health joked about my ability to still speak English after eleven years in a spanish speaking country. How absurd!

At the same time here were some Cuban specialists having the same degree as I did who could not speak English as well as I did but they were employed by the ministry. This I was briefed about by a high profile bureaucrat who sympathized with my plight. 'Doctor Toney this is not about your credentials, nor your ability to speak English or even about your documents not being translated. This is about you. You are not the son of an affluent businessman or some medical personality. Your degree means nothing to most persons of the status quo. If they cannot identify with your family as being part of the system you have no chance, you may not even be given the right to practise privately, you mark my words carefully, this is the nature of the beast here in capitalism." I got the picture and understood all the injustices that were being perpetuated against me, and mom finally disclosed to me, "I wanted you to fend for yourself as I see you are now a grown man. I know the Prime Minister personally and I can assist you. Arnhim Eustace is your relative and is slated to take over the reins of government when Sir James Mitchell resigns." I turned to her saying, "Bob Marley said, 'Never make a politician …… grant you a favour; they will always want …… to control you forever', If I can't get a job based on my qualifications, I do not wish any political job. How come I could be offered jobs all over the world as a specialist and in my own country which has a vacancy they are not willing to offer me the position? It's unfair." Mom continued to lecture me, "You see, people do not know you, they do not know your political affiliations. It shouldn't be so, but this is the reality in small 'impoverished' countries that are not socialist. You will have to take a crash course in capitalism," she joked.

It was heart rending and mind boggling to experience the abuses and vicious rumours about me, gross contempt, apathy and indifference shown to me. I was raging with fury and mom continued to lecture me about life and people. She said, "Great men and women are generally not born of or wanted by the system. Jesus Christ when he was born was never a part of the system. First he was from humble beginnings and was born in Bethlehem which was like saying he was from the worst place. He was conceived from a virgin, so they believed he was somebody else's child. He did carpentry (today some argue that it was building with stones, but that's beside the point whether or not he was a builder or carpenter). He wasn't part of the system, and the story goes on as you know it. This might just be the beginning of a great career in private practice."

And so I was allowed to practise medicine privately. Dr. Harold Rampersaud said to me, "Doc, you are allowed to practise medicine in any part of St. Vincent and the Grenadines from Fancy to Union Island, nobody can stop you." And it was so my practice started. I shook his hand and expressed my gratitude, cognizant of the fact that this was the closing chapter of the first stage of my life on becoming a doctor. I was legally allowed now to call myself Dr. Chester Toney M.D., specialist in Obstetrics and Gynaecology. This might have seemed insignificant to some persons, but to me it epitomized all the years of struggle, pain, suffering and tears and the confrontation with various professors for my true grades. It meant triumph of success over failure and as the saying goes, "The hotter the battle the sweeter the victory." I contemplated on the many persons who tried to stop this dream from being a reality. I remembered one teacher advising me to be more practical in my choice of profession after I had repeated the fourth form. She said, "You want to be a doctor and you have repeated. Why don't you think of something like agriculture seeing that you're from the country?" The only time in my life I felt discriminated against to the bone was in her class. She would put all of the repeaters on one side of the class and she would turn her back to us. "I have no time to spend on time wasters," she would say. We were not asked a single question for as she emphasized, "You all have missed your turn."

I reflected deeply on the words of professor Jose Oliva and Professor Nelson Rodriquez, my tutors in my four years of specialization. I remember Professor Oliva drilling into my head, "You are who you say you are. Never make anyone belittle your accomplishment."

"New Medicine"

Life Line Medical Clinic is the handiwork of my brother Adrian and me. We laboured from sun up to sun down doing the interior renovations of my clinic. We had some assistance though from Ali Browne, better known as the house husband and Brenzil Ashton. We did everything, interior decorations, choice of paint, layout and lighting. Adrian was a tower of strength in the materialization of my clinic. I started out optimistically ambitious. In hind sight if I'd known it would be so difficult, I might not have started in the first place. There were days when I saw no one and other days when I saw one person in the entire day, and as we would say in St. Vincent 'The dance couldn't pay for the light.'

I improvised in every aspect of my life and braced myself for the unthinkable; only God knows how I survived. I became an expert in digging a hole to fill a hole and juggling the dollars in those times of economic drought. Today, I can look back and smile, it was as though the hardship in Cuba had prepared me for this new life and I understood that God never gives you more than you can bear.

At Life Line Medical Clinic I try to adopt a pragmatic and realistic view of the severity of every case that confronts me. It is very essential that every physician gets to know his strengths and his weaknesses so that he can develop boundaries in his day to day practice. Any doctor worth his salt tries firstly to develop a relationship of trust with his patients; an experienced doctor knows that this will be the key to proceed. Building trust comes from a close observation of the patients within seconds. Building trust can mean making a joke or some other gesture which can make the patient feel comfortable, sometimes it's making an association with the person's name, age, address and possible family ties. These general details you will get from questioning the patient to know his/her clinical history. It's amazing how making association with the patients bridges the gap between the patient and the doctor. Language is the key in medicine, it's an advantage to speak the same language as the patient. You ought to know his or her social background and most of all their medical history. Such information is paramount when formulating your diagnosis or prescribing a course of treatment. At my clinic, I practise with an intimate relationship between conventional and alternative medicine. I can diagnose using certain alternative medicine modalities of diagnosis and I treat by conventional therapy or vice versa. Most doctors stick only to conventional medicine because that's what they've been taught at medical school. No fault of theirs, their convictions tell them that nothing else works, so they cannot be blamed wholly. If you have never seen a person being cured by alternative medicine then logically you will have no faith in such a practice. I'm of the opinion that a good doctor does not compromise with human life, some areas are totally out of bounds, that is to say, beyond the knowledge of a single doctor or health provider. So referrals should be encouraged when necessary. No doctor knows it all; this doesn't mean that you don't have to take risks as a physician but your risk should be based on your knowledge and experience and most importantly your own boundaries that only you alone know. In a nutshell you should be conscious about what you don't know.

Following the diagnosis you must devise a treatment which should strike a balance between getting the best results and creating the least possible harm. (All conventional drugs may have some harmful side effects). Here is where your knowledge of alternative medicine can make a difference. There is no perfect way of treating diseases. The doctor who believes that there is a perfect way in treating diseases can be considered ignorant. Do you know that no one knows the real reason with certainty why the human body becomes diseased? Your faith makes you pick a modality of treatment that has its own explanations for why we become sick. Think of it this way, if we knew the real reason for diseases then humanity would have been cured of all diseases. No one modality can treat all diseases in life. From my experience a certain percentage of alternative medicine and conventional medicine must be applied sometimes in combination, for instance acupuncture has solved many medical ailments. I have seen its use personally in the extraction of third molars, hysterectomy, thyroidectomy etc. This cannot be doubted. I've also seen acupuncture treat many ailments that conventional practitioners have not been able to resolve. Many physicians still see a conflict in combining alternative and conventional medicine where possible. There is only a conflict when money is your only objective.

Conventional medicine and alternative medicine need to merge to strengthen the possibility of saving lives. Western medical schools including those in Cuba, need to start adjusting the curricula to accommodate more alternative medicine modalities. Food and nutrition should be a specialty taught right throughout the curriculum instead of allocation of certain hours or months to its teaching. All forms of treatment of a patient should always, I repeat always be followed by dietary guidelines. Food that is necessary for your healing and food that is detrimental should always be accompanied by your treatment. I cannot over emphasize the link between emotions we cultivate which will put stress in your body and in the long run make you sick. Stress reduction goes hand in hand with the treatment you receive to promote healing ultimately. We believe in alternative medicine that every disease is caused by the ultimate result of toxemia. This encompasses everything that pollutes or lowers the body quantity or quality of oxygen which in the long run creates dysfunction.

Your body becomes toxic based on what you eat, emotions you cultivate, how much water you drink, (approximately eighty percent of the body is made up of water) and its quality, how much exercise and types of exercise you do in general, how you interact with nature or your environment in general. The closer you live with nature the fewer problems you have with nature.

Don't get me wrong, western or conventional medicine can provide you with a pacemaker which can eventually prolong life, but alternative medicine may be able to prevent you from having a heart problem in the first place. The combination of both alternative or complimentary medicine and conventional medicine is taking place more frequently today and the gap is finally closing. The combination of electronics and acupuncture known now as electro-acupuncture is being used extensively in the western world these days, so the future looks bright and many surgical operations are being done along with acupuncture. Before I conclude, I would like to touch one of the most controversial topics in western medicine, the consumption of milk and other pasteurized dairy products. Many conventional doctors still recommend milk as a daily part of your diet. The only milk that is recommended is that from a plant. This can include soya, coconut, sesame, vanilla and almond. We also recommend vanilla and soya once it is not genetically modified.

If you look at nature you will see that it is only the young mammal that drinks milk and it does so from its own species. It is only under domestication that dogs or cats will drink milk; if milk was so important to man, your mother will still produce milk even up to today for your consumption! It is an established fact that between one to ten percent of the calcium that enters your body from milk will be absorbed, the remaining ninety percent circulates as a toxic substance. Milk is one of the cheapest sources of calcium, phosphorus and magnesium. Have you ever heard the saying that cheap things are generally not good? On the other hand you can obtain calcium from vegetables like spinach, cabbage and other green leafy vegetables. More than ninety percent of the calcium found in these vegetables enters your body (good things aren't so cheap!) There are hundreds of experiments to confirm how harmful milk can be to the mature mammal (Dr. Pottinger's experiment is one of the most famous). You can see pasteurization of milk renders it very stable and it becomes hard to digest and even harder to excrete. In alternative medicine there's a general rule that you do not eat things that do not spoil quickly. Pasteurization of milk makes milk very difficult to spoil.

The exceptional case of Ricardo Woodley

Mr. Ricardo Woodley is employed with an international organization based in a European country. He has been working with this organization for the last twelve years. I am very humbled to have treated this distinguished Vincentian who has accomplished so much in his short life so far. Mr. Woodley is making a name for himself and St. Vincent and the Grenadines internationally.

Mr. Woodley turned up at my clinic one day in the summer of 2002. He complained that his right knee had been giving him 'some excruciating pain' for the last two years. I felt very honoured to be of service to him. Mr. Woodley who had then been in Europe for the past three years, in 2002 blamed the cold weather there where he shuttled between meetings and conferences. "I have seen several doctors there and my improvement has been dismal. I literally cry like a baby when pain strikes," he confessed. I have seen several orthopedic surgeons, nothing seems to work, nothing. I have done several tests with none being conclusive. Every test I did came back normal. I just cannot get out of bed at times, I cannot run anymore nor ride my bicycle, the knees just pain constantly."

I proceeded to examine him after asking him pertinent questions of his medical history. My clinical examination revealed that he was suffering from a condition called systematic Candidiasis. This is an entity which unfortunately your purely conventional doctor anywhere in the world can miss. Practitioners of alternative medicine know and can easily diagnose this condition. First of all, most purely conventional practitioners do not believe that this disease exists in a person who has been tested normal for yeast in the body. There is no real accurate test to date that can determine how much yeast you should have in your body. It boils down largely to the individual. Constituted science proclaims what you cannot prove is not scientific. So there you see why it may be so difficult to diagnose this condition. Most practitioners of alternative medicine know about the yeast test which is not accepted by conventional practitioners. Mr. Woodley became agitated on hearing my diagnosis. "I've been prescribed many anti-inflammatory drugs for years, could these contribute to my problem?" he asked. I went on to explain that over exposure to so many conventional drugs had caused an overgrowth of yeast cells in his body and that the tests he did would not reflect this easily. I was able to conclude this because of my experience treating other patients, I explained. I devised a regimen to replenish the intestinal flora in his body and also to detoxify his body and ordered a change of diet, more so to eliminate the yeast forming food such as pasteurized milk, refined starch and sugar, animal protein and carbonated beverages. Mr. Woodley returned to Europe and called within two weeks to update me on his progress. "I am ninety percent better", he remarked. "It's miraculous, I am walking without any signs of a limp, my knee is without any pain, I'm running for longer distances." I then enquired about his orthopedic surgeon and asked if he had given him the good news. "My doctor laughed heartily when I told him about the treatment you had given to me and even went as far as asking if I was sure that you were a physician," he said.

"He suggested that the problem could have been caused by climatic changes in the first place. Since this regimen of treatment my knee has proven to be just fine. I had not suffered like this in life before Doc, I am living testimony that your style of medicine has some success even when everything else failed."

I've been deeply humbled by his comment and I reflected upon how simple treatments can touch the lives of others and make their lives more comfortable and meaningful.

Earl 'Ole George' Daniel and Joel Butcher

Supervising four times the unofficial record holders Earl 'Ole George' Daniel and Joel Butcher is an achievement I would cherish during my lifetime. For me it represents the epitome of all my struggles with all my scars to show. My battle against prodigious odds, the sacrifice that a 'country boy' had made in his lifetime to deny his detractors the opportunity to prove that I didn't have what it takes to make a difference in the world.

Ole George and Joel Butcher will go down in history as great men whether or not the Guinness Book of World records accepts it; history is history and that cannot change. The international press has seen them in action and that is recorded as world history. In the history books of our country it will be highlighted that these two men did something that no other persons ever did before, but like so many of our heroes before they were overlooked based upon some legal technicality. This reminds me of a sonnet - The Truth Or The Law? by a Vincentian poet Ardon Nelson, "*Oh truth, it's always shameful when your great treaty, Is broken by a legal technicality.*"

"I challenge the Guinness book of records to accept any one of the walks or all if they may so that our children and grandchildren will not judge us as persons who contributed nothing to humanity. The Guinness book of world records' judgment or lack thereof will always be viewed as an unfair ruling against a small nation state and more importantly two of its bravest citizens. These two walking heroes deserve equal respect and recognition for their outstanding courage and determination never before seen in human history.

The world record is not of tremendous significance to me personally, but to black people worldwide. What intrigues me as a medical practitioner is the journey traversed by Earl 'Ole George' Daniel from being a sick person visiting my clinic in 2000 to a healthy strong individual who would defy all odds and break four world records.

Even though he has not been recognized by the Guinness book of world records officially, I know we have made an indelible contribution to mankind in the field of perseverance. His records will be very hard to beat. He is a Vincentian hero, a walking hero of the entire world and we as a people are very proud of his achievements.

When 'Ole George' walked into my office in March of 2000, he said that he was having severe pain in his jaw and stated frankly that he was having no redress using conventional therapies and that he was willing to try something else. "Something more natural," he emphasized. "I saw on your sign that you practise alternative medicine also, so I'm interested to know if you can help me. I have had some advance reports and recommendation from someone you have treated and I'm here hoping you can help me." I asked pertinent questions of his clinical history and began to examine him and in about fifteen minutes I was able to formulate his diagnosis.

It was a rare condition. "I cannot understand how the doctors in Canada could have missed this," he said. I consoled him by assuring him that maybe they had diagnosed his condition but may not have explained it to him. I tried to calm him down by saying, "It's my knowledge of chiropractic adjustments that I used to confirm the diagnosis. I can send you for an x-ray, CT scan or even MRI, but there's no need to, once this test is positive. He looked at me in amazement and said, "Dr. Toney, I don't know if what you are telling me is true or false you know, but you are persuading me. I did all these tests in Canada, how come nothing showed up?" I smiled and replied, "There is no perfect system of diagnosing or healing. Modern medicine is just a few hundred years old. People were being treated for this ailment for thousands of years using alternative medicine. That was before there was CAT scan, MRI etc. Some argue that different versions of these existed then as there is nothing new under the sun." After an adjustment he said, "Doc, it's the best I've felt in the last five years, I can't believe this thing works so fast." I outlined some exercises he should perform on a daily basis, some emotional cleansing, some dietary adjustments and an ionized bracelet regimen. I also ordered a detoxification programme. I observed his progress the next month when he returned. He had improved by leaps and bounds. He confessed that running on the beach, swimming, along with his daily intake of fruits and vegetables that I had advised him to eat had helped him tremendously to overcome his ailment. He was so excited over his progress that he emphatically stated, "I feel like I could walk around St. Vincent."

At first I thought he was using exaggeration for emphasis to give a visual image of how much he had improved, then he said, "Doc, you not listening to me you know." Then I thought he was having withdrawal syndrome from the detoxification I ordered. It also dawned on me at the same time that he was joking because he is also a stand up comedian. I looked at him in amazement wondering if he was really sane. I began smiling so that he would not recognize that I doubted his statement. "Doctor Toney I know you must be thinking that I'm going mad, but I'm not. I have intentions of breaking the world record for the longest continuous walk without sleep and I've chosen you to assist me. You have proven to me that you are the doctor most qualified to supervise my preparations and the monitoring of the walk." To date it was one of the most difficult responses that I have ever had to give to any patient. "I want us to take on the world, you with your 'knowledge' and I with my willpower and inner strength, we can make a world record breaking combination. Are you ready?" I replied, "Yes I'm ready." And it was so that the idea was born. I cautioned him, but I was prepared to help him in his quest for success in breaking the world record. I remember cautioning him about the program which entailed months of physical and mental preparations. His preparations included constant examinations and monitoring of physical and mental endurance tests, building mental toughness, managing social issues such as criticism from the press and how to socialize with various communities bearing in mind each community's socio-political composition along the walk.

We coordinated with the trainer James Bentick who I consider to be one of the finest in the world. We had our debates, both James and I. Looking back I know he would say that these heated encounters paid great dividends. James can be considered an eclectic professional. He is level headed, calm in adversity with a penetrating intelligence seldom seen in sportsmen, including administrators of the discipline. His trademark quality to me will always be his curious mind and penetrating exercises that he ordered for 'Ole George'. No wonder he was coach of the year of St. Vincent and the Grenadines once and three times senior sportsman of the year. It shows that my own analysis of James is not biased or based on my friendship with him. I will go on record as saying that the four official world records established by 'Ole George' and Joel Butcher could not have been possible without his assistance if this distinguished Vincentian coach who represented St. Vincent in the Commonwealth games in squash in Melbourne in 2006, was not involved.

I pursued a refresher course in "dehydration" and "rehydration" along with hydro-mineral balances in the human body. When all the preparations were finished we were ready to take on this humongous task. In fact we were pursuing a task that was unknown to anybody in the world; we were venturing into virgin territory. The world was now our stage and St. Vincent and the Grenadines was now the space chosen to perform our act. So it was lights, camera and we were off.

We set out six days before the 14th of March 2005. Our goal was to culminate this walk on National Heroes day, 14th March. I checked 'Ole George' and Joel Butcher for dehydration, and had blood pressure and pulse monitoring at various intervals so as to guarantee their safety health wise. I was meticulous in the food that they consumed during the walk, intervening personally in what type of food and liquid they should have. I had always instructed them on the severity of the walk and warned that without proper preparation of the body and mind through proper nutrition that their bodies could shut down instantly in the grueling task of walking for six days continuously without sleeping.

We had established before the walk that if I had any reservation at any time about continuing the walk it would be announced publicly, so that in the event of any medical complications I would not be held accountable. There was a moment when I wanted to give up and withdraw my expertise from the group. I had commented to my mom that I was willing to throw in the towel as I was becoming fearful for the lives of the two men. My colleagues in the medical profession were convinced that these two were mad men and they had gotten me involved in their madness. "You are not exercising good judgment as a physician," one physician scolded, "Do you know if something were to happen to these men the medical board of St. Vincent could revoke your licence to practise?" I started experiencing cold feet and mom consoled me, "Winners never quit and quitters never win," she said. "I looked at these two men on TV walking and the Lord told me that they will make it." I trusted her judgment more than any human being that I knew and she continued, "The Lord has told me that this will be the beginning of a whole new life for you, be brave and face the challenges head on." I was obliged. As a medical doctor, sometimes you doubt your scientific capabilities to perform the task. I had done the pertinent research, interfaced online and via telephone with some of my professors and other experts in the field. This may surprise you but nobody, absolutely no professor either in Cuba or America had ever ventured in this field before. They were advising me based on their experiences on marathons. My confidence had grown since we conceptualized the idea of breaking the world record of six days of walking continuously. The moment was approaching. On 13th March 2005 at 1p.m., tragedy struck; Joel Butcher was reported to have experienced a bout of stupor, an elevation in his blood pressure, more so the systolic reading had risen by 10mm Hg (mercury) compared to all the previous readings. His blood pressure was now 130/80. I then made the decision that if his blood pressure remained the same at 8 in the morning, I would withdraw my services as the physician responsible for him.

At 8:00 that morning, I checked both men. Ole George's vital signs were perfect, however he showed signs of moderate exhaustion. On the other hand, Joel Butcher did not show signs of exhaustion but was nursing an injury to his right ankle, an injury sustained when he stepped into a pothole the night before. I was particularly concerned that Joel Butcher's blood pressure had remained at 130/80. I somehow was concerned about the injury to his right ankle and so I decided that I would not be responsible if anything were to happen. I explained, "You will be walking on your own from now onwards, I'm advising you to desist from walking." The press carried my statement live and I was bombarded with a series of criticisms. "The doctor does not want Joel Butcher to end the walk, he wants Ole George to do so alone because he's close to Ole George; boy this doctor bad minded!"

This was very far from the truth. I knew I was going to clinch victory out of the jaws of defeat and it was just a matter of time. Victory is always surrounded by conflict and contradiction. In this walk I had explored all the parameters of homeostasis which deals with mainly normal body function while facing adverse conditions. Armed with this scientific knowledge and the commitment of the walkers to perform such an improbable task, I was now relieved at the end of the walk. Ole George and Joel Butcher had done it. They had surprisingly broken the world record and had walked for six days and twenty three minutes. There was an incredible number of persons in the streets of Kingstown. Some estimated that there were close to twenty thousand persons there who had travelled from every nook and cranny of St. Vincent to cheer on their local heroes, home boy Joel Butcher and Earl 'Ole George' Daniel. Persons lined the streets of Kingstown to get a glimpse of these two walking heroes. Hurray we had done it! St. Vincent and the Grenadines was now a nation of hard core perseverance and endurance walkers. I had represented the scientific and medical community of St. Vincent and the Grenadines and the world over, and I felt honoured. Bingo! I had personally hit the mark at that moment, nothing that anyone had done to me in the past mattered. I had forgiven all of my enemies. I pondered on the unfair denial of a job in the land of my birth; the land that I loved so much and cherished dearly and nothing that my enemies did unjustly to me was of any relevance. I felt the pieces fall into place and I knew then the reason why the Lord had designed things to happen the way they did.

I said, "Thank you Lord for your blessings on me, you saw I deserved this." After a very touching address by various persons including the Prime Minister Hon. Dr. Ralph Gonsalves and the opposition leader Hon. Arhim Eustace, I took both men to the Milton Cato Memorial Hospital. I was amazed both men remained in good health. All that was left to do now was to contact the Guinness Book of World records for endorsement. Unfortunately, we learnt later that Guinness did not approve of this and every Vincentian was saddened. Since then, Earl 'Ole George' Daniel and Joel Butcher have broken three more unofficial world records in endurance walking. No other person has done this in living memory. This incredible feat of walking for seven days one hour was also completed in Jamaica.

The walk in Jamaica was done in 2006 and publicized a great deal. We attracted many sponsors who were placing their monies where their mouths were in supporting these Vincentian superstars. The walk took place in Emancipation Park and unfortunately Joel Butcher was unable to complete the walk due to an injury he sustained during the process. 'Ole George' single handedly took the challenge to task and completed the walk in six days, one hour. The government and people of Jamaica celebrated and congratulated him on this mammoth achievement. I was excited on his achievement as his physician, but saddened due to the fact that I was not physically there to care for him and to see with my own eyes, history repeated under my stewardship. It was time for the Guinness Book of World Records again to place our efforts in the history books. This again was not meant to be, Guinness was not willing to acknowledge our achievements.

Let's reflect on what has happened so far. In the first submission, the Guinness Book of World Records stated that there was disparity in the terrain of St. Vincent and the Grenadines and the park where the record was set. In the second submission which was in Jamaica, they never replied; or if they did I am not aware.

The third submission which was done in St. Vincent again in 2007 was not acknowledged. In this one, he repeated the same route traversed in the same walk, but this time he walked for seven days and one hour. I prepared and supervised this walk. Not daunted by Guinness's lack of acknowledgement, Ole George returned to my office again and said, "It seems like they don't want to acknowledge the walk because it was not done in a developed country, well I want to walk in Central Park. I am getting some assistance from the Rotary Club in St. Vincent along with Vincentians living in New York. I'm fully prepared to go the extra mile Doc." So it was that Ole George and Joel Butcher walked again in Central Park in August 2008. This time he had all the international press coverage that one can envisage in the United States, I was not there to supervise him medically but we kept in contact by telephone. Once again Ole George did the unthinkable. He walked for eight days in the right place, the city that never sleeps and broke his world record once again, but the Directors of the Guinness Book of World Record were not troubled. Ole George and Butcher are heroes, they are true Vincentian and Caribbean heroes and as my brother Cephus puts it, "Guinness wants them to become ill or crazy or die trying!"

It's incredible how such an established and influential company can withhold a legacy of these two great men and also the Vincentian nation of its rightful place in world history. Guinness, you can take any one of those four walks and include them in your record books. Until that day the struggle continues persistently while our people await the result of your judgment. Until that day, I will remain a thorn in your side until you decide to right this historical wrong.

The fearless spirit of our paramount chief Joseph Chatoyer lives in the heart of Ole George and Joel Butcher and by extension all our people; this unwavering perseverance and un-relenting strength of chief Chatoyer lives in the blood of all our people which is reflective of our deep rooted patriotism and deep nationalism. I am just advocating the desires of our people to be free from the injustice perpetuated by the Guinness Book of World Records. When the Directors of Guinness wake on mornings and look in the mirror I want them to be cognizant of the fact that they have denied an entire nation a place in world history, and from this day onwards, many Vincentians will champion the cause of Ole George and Joel Butcher, true sons of our Vincentian nation.

Chapter 11

Overcoming My Battles With Caffeine And Nicotine Addiction

Professor Robert Añe Aquilochi of internal medicine once reported to me that he was asked by a South African, "Why do Cubans smoke so much?" He replied, "When Christopher Columbus discovered Cuba, the first thing he saw was an Indian smoking tobacco dressed in loincloth. This dangerous habit we have taught the world, so it is no coincidence that we are one of the top tobacco and cigarette smoking countries in the world."

This in part explains my unfortunate use of cigarettes and caffeine in Cuba. The availability of cigarettes laid the foundation for my addiction. Culturally Cuba is a nation that consumes coffee excessively. People express their gratitude with a cup of coffee, they have casual drinks with coffee, coffee is an integral part of the Cuban's day to day culture. It is this custom of the Cuban people that anyone, I repeat anyone who comes to your home should be offered a drink of coffee. Most people who smoke try to accompany smoking with a drink of coffee.

I took my first real puff on a cigarette in 1988 while sharing a room with a chain smoker from Sierra Leone and three Panamanians who were also smokers. I remember one of the students giving me my first lesson on how to smoke a cigarette. As a novice I started coughing and so it began. One puff led to another then before I knew it, I was carrying my own pack of cigarettes in my pocket. Smoking became a habit along with increased consumption of coffee. In Cuba every student at that time, whether you smoked or not was given thirty packs of cigarettes, a custom I never agreed with, but at the same time I understood its rationale. Those who didn't smoke could sell these cigarettes for twice their monthly stipend, and those who smoked had no reason to take their stipend and support their habit. In a sense it meant indulging in black market activities to support a smoking habit as some students related when they got in trouble with the Cuban authorities. So you can imagine with the availability of cigarettes and a young growing habit of drinking coffee, I was well on the way to becoming an addict to these two substances. Most of all though, it was my inability to handle stress at that time that perpetuated my need to smoke. It was also my great desire to be on top of any situation and it was from here I began smoking and drinking my life away with cigarette in my right hand and coffee in the left; and I vowed these two provided the ammunition that made me ready to confront the world.

Those persons who have never smoked will ask the question, why do doctors smoke when they know how harmful it is to them. My response will be, doctors smoke even though they are armed with the knowledge of the dangers it can cause to your health because they want to save lives, that is to say, by smoking they feel more alert, they feel more equipped to make decisions. At least that is how the drugs make you feel and you tell yourself that it's necessary for you to think clearly so that you don't make mistakes with people's lives. I know that you will find it very ironic and senseless, but this is the conclusion that I came to while I was a smoker working very hard in the hospitals, performing three or four c-sections in one night, coupled sometimes with an emergency of an ectopic pregnancy or a hysterectomy; because one has to be performing at one's peak when dealing with human lives, this puts great stress on the physician.

Professor Nelson Rodriquez, one of Cuba's pioneers in Laparoscopic surgery in Gynaecology noted the severity of my smoking habit, "Doctor Toney when you are in the business of saving people's lives, you should start saving yours first," he remarked. He had awoken in me a different way of thinking from then on, but I was so engulfed in the habit that just the thought of quitting made me ill. I then realized that I had opened up myself to these demons that had overpowered me and were getting the better of me. I smoked two packs of 'Popular' cigarettes per day (these are some of the strongest cigarettes in the world) made in Cuba. This I've been told by many foreigners who have smoked with me. This may sound incredible or even inconceivable, but I would become constipated if I did not smoke or have a drink of coffee.

Nicotine and caffeine were now a part of my body's physiology and they were choking me to death slowly. They were tricking me into believing that if I did not smoke I would die, but whenever I tried to stop my body seemed as though it was malfunctioning. I attempted to quit about five times but it was the most difficult undertaking, for I could not operate surgically at the pace to which I was accustomed.

My habit grew very offensive to some of my close non-smoking friends, but I could not help it and it seemed as though the urge increased with each pack. I remember once, while in Jamaica, I took a taxi from Norman Manley International Airport to go to St.Catherine 69 Canal Drive, Portmore, where two of my good friends Pamitra Blackman and George Nelson lived, but halfway along the journey, I felt the great desire to smoke, so I asked the taxi driver if I could smoke in his car and he said yes. I proceeded to smoke my Cuban 'popular' cigarettes. The taxi driver suddenly stopped, the tyres making a screeching noise, I thought we had almost had an accident when he came out of the car, opened the passenger door and said, "Out ah me car star! Out!" "What happen?" I asked, "In my twenty years as a taxi driver, me never carry no man 'inna' my car smoking ganja yet," he stormed. I politely explained that it was not marijuana, but it was Cuba's 'Popular' cigarette which was so distinct in smell from most of the others that we sometimes smoked, cigarettes like Salem, Moore, Camel, Malboro and 555.

The closest cigarette in smell and strength to the Cuban 'popular' that I have smoked is Gitano, a French cigarette. The taxi driver calmed down and apologized to me. "Man da cigarette almost smell like ganja. How I saw no filter at the end, I mistook it for marijuana."

I smoked Cuban cigars at times, these are rated as some of the world's finest. It's amazing how such expensive products were always available at my home. I had patients who regularly gave me cigars of the finest quality, Coheiba, Romeo y Julieta Davidoff to name a few. Sometimes I smoked them; at times I would take them to Jamaica to give some of my friends there. These cigars have often helped me in my hour of dire need when I was low on finance and had to trade them in return for commodities to take back to Cuba.

When I returned as a specialist to St. Vincent, I believed that I would enter the job market immediately as I had already been promised a job with the government and also the fact that I had borrowed monies from the government bank to self finance my studies. I returned 17th September 1998 and I'd only bought one month's supply of cigarettes, so when all my supplies ran out, I knew I was in Filth Street. I went into having early withdrawal symptoms (from headaches, mental confusion, tiredness, insomnia, palpitation) you name it, I had it. I had no money to support the habit and my mom was not prepared to assist me in this area. Then I had to apply my knowledge of alternative medicine to treat it. I took high doses of Vitamin C along with Calcium and Magnesium. I also used Braggs Apple Cider Vinegar and Tisane de Durban. My recovery was slow with nightmares every night. I suffered intensely, eleven years of caffeine and nicotine consumption had ended and I vowed never to touch a cigarette or drink a cup of coffee again. This I've adhered to since 1999.

It is said that you are never out of the woods once you have suffered some form of substance abuse or other forms of addiction. The psychologist argues that forty percent of any addiction had an environmental origin. I strongly believe that this is so and I know if I was still living in an environment like Cuba which I had lived in for eleven years and many of my colleagues still smoked and drank coffee, it would have been virtually impossible for me to kick these habits. It has not been smooth sailing, for these demons still follow me around even after eleven years. However, I've been able to conquer them. What prevents me from touching a cigarette or taking another cup of coffee are the vivid images still etched in my memory of the discomfort I experienced during my withdrawal syndrome. I would like to state categorically that I would not wish such a state of discomfort on my worst enemy.

Sometimes I try to visualize how difficult it must be for those persons hooked on much harder drugs like cocaine, crystal methamphetamines', heroin, LSD and even alcohol. After all nicotine and caffeine are still babies in comparison to these harsher drugs.

At the end of the day the best way to overcome these addictions is to stay away from them in the first place and if you have succeeded in quitting, then keep away from persons who indulge in similar practices and try to reflect on the biblical scriptures, 'Your body is the temple of the Lord'. This will go a long way in reinforcing your convictions to stay drug free.

You become a slave to your addictions. I recall in the midst of 'special period' (a post perestroika era when the Soviet Union cut trade with Cuba by eighty percent. This name was given to this period by the Cuban Government to connote conditions of war in times of peace) cigarettes went very scarce and the price surged from four pesos to a hundred pesos per pack. Our stipend per month was sixty pesos. The price for everything went up. There were prices of war in times of peace. Many Cubans began to blame the United States embargo on the island for the state of dire hardship. It was in this time in Cuba that many avid businessmen made a kill in business. Words cannot explain the level of scarcity there was at that time. Many students hooked on this addiction of nicotine or coffee, traded clothes, jewelry and appliances etc to feed the habit. Many of the Caribbean students who smoked became closer and operated like a commune to tackle the harsh reality; and we had to bail out one another when the going got rough. I thank God that today I don't have to throw away my earnings to support such a dreadful and dangerous habit. I still ask the Lord to strengthen me and prevent me from going back there again; I surely cannot afford another relapse.

Secret lessons from my love life

It's not very often that one reads about the secrets of one's past. In fact while discussing the idea with a close friend of mine, I was warned that the idea was not wise and that I should refrain from writing about this part of my life for it might get me into 'deep hot waters'. I contemplated for many months but I was unable to adhere to his advice. I could not resist the temptation and I also believed my book would be incomplete without mentioning the persons whom I've been very close to and the impact they have made upon my life and my personality. I'm about to reveal some inside secrets of my love life in Cuba. Some of these relationships have helped to mould me into the person I am today and to omit them would be like erasing the foundation of who I am, even the essence of this book.

Over the years, I have developed an understanding of the opposite sex through deep friendships and serious love relationships. Some of these relationships on their own may be worthy of a novel, perhaps a documentary or even a movie. I do not seek to be ostentatious at this juncture, but I do believe that I have had quite an exciting experience which has given me a view of the opposite sex that I would consider broader than the average man. I reflect on the long period spent in the Republic of Cuba and sometimes I really do ask myself, did I really spend eleven years there? Then I would pinch myself remembering a famous quotation that I learnt in Cuba, "Time goes by slowly when you are waiting on it, quickly when you are having fun, and it lasts a thousand years when you are in love, and it ceases to exist when you die."

The experiences I have gained with respect to the opposite sex were immense and have helped to shape my own philosophy toward women that I have coined using my own expression when it comes to dealing with them (No hard feelings to you women) 'Women, difficult to live with but I don't want to be in any world without them." I've drawn the conclusion that any man that lives in this world and is not motivated by a woman has actually ceased to live, he has only existed. I've also learnt that women tend to be the same wherever you go. Their needs, dreams and aspirations differ slightly around the edges but remain the same at the core. Stevie Wonder summarizes this in his song "Ebony and Ivory", "We all know that people are the same where ever you go, there is good and bad in everyone." I once met a ninety five year old Jamaican man who was living in Cuba for sixty years. It was 1991 to be exact. He told me, "Son, there are three things that man should have to maintain a good relationship with a woman. (1) He must have a good relationship of mutual respect and love; (2) he must have money or some material possession that makes a woman feel secure; and (3) these two go hand in hand, you can't separate them, good sex and a little argument sometimes."

I was somewhat astonished at the time. I had never heard or read anything like this before. I use it as a guide up to this day and I've always kept it to the back of my head. I have always understood that romance is the oil that lubricates a relationship, especially the long term ones; however I have come to the conclusion that women look at men as providers in the broadest sense. This is to say, a man should be able to provide a woman with most of her desires. If he's not able now she may be hopeful that one day he will be able to do so. Men tend to look at women as their caretaker. Their roles are generally reflected in the man's mind similar to those of the mother and in the woman's mind similar to her father. It doesn't matter how educated you become, the bottom line remains. You are basically still man or woman and this intrinsic desire does not change and the law of supply and demand still plays a significant role in determining the outcome of relationships.

All my relationships with the opposite sex, even the shortest, have had great significance to me and have contributed to my formulation of an understanding of women. It is generally said that it is only women who truly understand women. But as my mom used to tell me, "God never asked men to understand women, he just asked them to love them." It just seems impossible for a man to totally understand women and vice versa. I have tried to understand them drawing on my experiences as a gynaecologist to comprehend their femininity and charm with their intermittent emotional turmoil so reflective in their cyclical behaviour. In fact, no man can truly understand a woman without first understanding the essence of her menstrual cycle. It is the basis of understanding the female biologically, psychologically and socially. I have had many heated discussions with some liberal and feminist personalities who have differed from this point of view. But I believe that I'm not too far off from being right as I'm able to see women in a different way because of my profession.

I think I have even acquired a greater understanding of my masculinity, it's purpose, value and effect on the female world. I came to the realization that when masculinity is blended with confidence and preconceived virility in a woman's mind, it evokes an effect upon the female which is sometimes interpreted as male 'virility'. I can't help but mention Omar Sharif's statement, "All virile men become close to the female world." I know I have charmed some of the world's most beautiful women in my lifetime. Many of them could have won Miss World or Miss Universe, and just like Julio Iglesias I say, thanks, "To all the girls I have loved before."

In synthesis I have grown to interpret the genitalia of both male and female as being symbolic of their own sexuality. The female genitalia (vagina) extend from outside to inside. This symbolizes the depth of her sexuality and emotions. This is to say her feelings may start from outside and extend profoundly to the inside. It also confers a sense of mystery about the female. She reasons a lot more profoundly than the average male with respect to love and sexuality. On the other hand the male genitalia is very superficial extending mostly outwards, this symbolizing his level of commitment, his emotions and sexuality. This is not an attempt to justify the frequently uncommitted tendencies of the male, but an attempt to highlight his weaknesses in his sexuality and emotions which tend to explain in part why when the average man sees a lady that he considers beautiful or sexy, it doesn't matter much, her level of education, her image of the world, he is moved by her physically and this is considered very important in starting and maintaining a relationship. He also starts formulating in his mind how she may look in certain sexual positions. This may cause many women to feel cheap at times but it's a reality about the male that you can't change so easily. I know you would like him to think more about your family background, your values as a woman etc, but this generally does not occur like that with the average male and you would have to gamble sometimes that if you take a person who does not conform to the psychology of the average male, you may run the risk that you end up with an unsatisfied love life. In my pre-clinical years, my professor of embryology referred to the fact that the average man has the capacity to impregnate all the women in Cuba and by extension the USA. If you were to individually isolate each sperm cell that he may possess (a normal sperm count of the average male is between 20 million and 160 million –volume). It sounds freaky doesn't it? The fact that a woman produces only one egg per month means that she would be more meticulous generally with whom she mates just in case conception should occur. She tends to protect and guard jealously this egg while on the other hand a man produces so many sperm; he tends to be more irrational about where he sows his seeds.

I would not finish without highlighting what I believe is the formula for success in relationships. I believe that love is the most important ingredient in any relationship. I have devised a formula based on my own experiences and the experiences of many couples with whom I came into contact. It is not a formula that I have seen in any text book nor my classes in sexology. Any similarity to this formula is pure coincidence.

It is called Love = Power x Money x Sex.

L = PMS (not premenstrual syndrome).

These are crucial factors that determine a relationship. Power will refer to the decisive role being played in a relationship; in other words who calls the shots. It is also understood as who is accepted to make the major decisions in the home. Money is defined as economic security in a general sense. It is generally not limited to hard currency, it can also mean material possessions.

Sex is understood as the inter-relationship, whether physical or emotional between two persons of the opposite sex. It also involves how, where, and when the sex act is performed. When there is the absence of one or more components of this formula in any given relationship, problems arise that threaten the continuation of the relationship. Disaster strikes when there is an absence of all three! It was Bernard Iddengs Bell who said, "It is good that man should think; but it is indispensable that men should love." Here I am about to reveal some of the secrets of my love life. These have never been shared with anyone before.

Maria

Maria was a beautiful 'Mulatta' who I had met in Rancho Luna restaurant in Camagüey while I was learning Spanish in 1987. She was considered to have a Coca Cola shape with a radiant smile, a perfect ten. She was just irresistible, that's no lie, a perfectly shaped lady she was; and she was accompanied by her cousin Norma. After introduction I asked permission to sit with these two beauties. I was still battling with my Spanish and struggled to appear fluent. I was practically regurgitating my Spanish classes and both Maria and Norma thought that I was funny. "I am from St. Vincent and the Grenadines, my name is Chester, I am a medical student, I am presently studying Spanish at this time, afterwards I will study medicine, and you?" They introduced themselves to me and were killing themselves with laughter. Maria concluded that my accent was just stunning and she made me blush. "Oh you have chestnut eyes," she replied and I felt like I was in cloud nine. It was one of the first times in my entire life that I felt conscious about my eyes. At least I could not remember anyone in the past, especially girls commenting on the colour of my eyes. Instantly I felt close to her from that time onwards and my passion for her grew uncontrollably. She had given me her address and I became very interested in visiting her. "You can visit me anytime, just call me first," she said boldly. I was very excited about her invitation and decided that nothing would stop me from following up. In fact, I was guilty of not following up on many offers made to me in the past to visit girls' homes. Maybe it was the way I was brought up as a child; however I could not resist this invitation which had gotten the better of me.

I started visiting Maria's home to talk to her and her grand parents welcomed me with open arms. She had an uncle who coincidentally was a gynaecologist and professor at Camaguey medical school, Dr. Antonio Ruz who insisted that I call him Toni. He was one of the most humble professionals that I had ever met. He spoke passionately about his profession and spoke perfect Spanish. He instructed me to learn as much as I could to go back to my country. Maria blushed every now and then and I would give her a 'sweet eye' when her uncle was not watching me. He had impressed me with his command of the Spanish language and his meticulous explanations of the new discoveries in Gynaecology. Looking back now after so many years, I think Toni must have influenced my decision to choose Gynaecology as my specialty. I was surprised though when he changed the topic and started to state some facts about St. Vincent and the Grenadines. He stated, "Your country is the only seasonal whaling country in the Caribbean and if I'm not wrong in the entire Western Hemisphere." He continued by expressing his knowledge of La Soufriere Volcano, one of the most monitored in the world. He also spoke of the botanical gardens, the oldest in the western hemisphere, which was established in 1765. It was amazing how a gynaecologist knew that the Grenadine islands are some of the finest yachting destinations in the world and one of the best places for snorkeling. He knew that the Amazona guildingii, St. Vincent's parrot was indigenous to St. Vincent. At this point, Maria was excited about all her uncle was relating to me and jokingly asked me, "Will you invite me to your country one day for a vacation? I'm falling in love with your country." I answered, "Well, well, well, such a coincidence, you are falling in love with my country and I am falling in love with you." Everyone in the house laughed simultaneously as though they were watching a comedy. I felt very relaxed and appreciated. Maria lived with her grand parents and Norma. Her mom and dad had migrated to the USA. Her uncle Toni who visited her frequently did not waste any time in officially extending a warm welcome to me. "Chester, you are officially welcomed to our home, you can come when you want to, we see you appreciate Maria, if it's reciprocal you have my blessings. I don't know about my mother and father." Her grandfather Pancho cleared his throat and replied, "Well, I am from the old school and I would like Mr. Toney to write us a letter explaining his intentions with our granddaughter to date, someone who can read and write Castellano, after all he is still studying the language." Maria got furious. "No Chester, any letter you write you write to me. My grandfather doesn't understand that this is the modern times, he still lives in the past. If we get to the point where we are dating and we appreciate each other, that's our business." It was the first time I had seen her so decisive and confident. "You didn't talk Maria, you preached" replied Norma. From that time onwards I dated Maria and everything was just right. We spent weekends together on Santa Lucia beach… you should have seen yours truly basking in the Cuban sun in Hawaiian shirts with sunglasses enjoying a slice of paradise in the land of song, sea and sun. I also frequented Nuevitas when we were not visiting Santa Lucia sometimes we went to Guimaro and Brasilia where she had many relatives.

Maria dropped out of law school in the final year and anytime we had an argument she would say, "Listen Doc, I am a trained lawyer without a law degree, you must listen to me." Sometimes I could not come to grips with her liberal way of seeing the world. She was very humorous and shared many interesting jokes about lawyers with me. She told me about a lawyer who once went to the funeral of a very prominent businessman in the community. Everyone agreed that they would contribute something while his body was lying in the coffin. They put hundreds of dollar notes in the coffin and when it was the lawyer's turn to make a contribution, in fact he waited for last, then he counted the money that was there and publicly exclaimed that he would double it. They had donated the sum of five thousand dollars and fifty cents. The lawyer wrote a cheque for ten thousand dollars and signed his name and telephone number at the back and putting it in the coffin, the money the others had donated in his wallet, then made the sign of the cross. "May you rest in peace," he said then retreated.

She asked me a riddle that an English lawyer had once asked her while he was visiting the law school. "What happens to lawyers after they die?" I was dumbfounded and couldn't get the answer, then she replied, "They lie still." We really shared some wonderful times together. She reminded me that lawyers and doctors are similar some ways, and she was the first to highlight to me that we both save lives in one way of the other; for going to jail is no life. Her grandfather Pancho was quite an interesting character. He grew to like me a lot and I became another member of the family during my year in Camagüey.

Then I was chosen to study medicine in Havana and so we became separated. My first year in medical school was so intense that I was unable to return to see her as I should and when she came to visit me, I was so busy that we had very little time for each other and as the old folks say, out of sight out of mind. We drifted out of love eventually. I understand that she returned to law school and completed her law degree. The last time I heard from her she was working as a lawyer in Camagüey.

Chavela

I met Chavela in San Miguel del pardon where I visited frequently to see some friends who lived in Reparto Monterry. She worked at the neurosurgical institute which wasn't too far from the hospital I attended; hospital Comandante Manuel Fajardo. We were on a bus and I saw her watching me curiously as though she knew me before. I could not resist asking her, so I bravely approached her on the bus while we were both standing. "Did I meet you before?" I asked and she laughed heartily and replied, "That's the oldest line in the book." Her smile was as wide as the river Nile. "I don't know but I've seen you passing on your way to your hospital. I am a nurse by profession and I work at the Institute of neurosurgery and neurology on street 29 between F and G." I was surprised that she knew me. Coincidentally both of us disembarked at the same bus stop. She said, "I live about five blocks down that street." So I asked her, "Can I come to your hospital to see you?" She replied, "The only problem is that I'm usually very busy, but if you stop by, I can squeeze a little time in to say hi!" She was polite and simple and apparently very kind, and her infectious smile remains in my mind up to this day.

She was very beautiful and dressed very modestly. We were able to share a long relationship which underlying qualities were respect and love. Chavela was a great fan of Vincy music. She knew many of the songs from St. Vincent by heart and was impressed with the high quality of music coming out of my country. She even reported that she showered with the music of the band 'Touch' in the background.

She liked the infectious lyrics of songs like, 'Kangaroo', 'Man can't tek butt', 'Back off' and 'Maco'. She felt that she could never get enough of our internationally famous Alston 'Beckett Cyrus's songs, 'Ten years', 'Teaser', 'Ah war soca', and 'Gel ah rush me'. Chavela often introduced her friends and relatives to St. Vincent's music and they also were impressed with the high quality and depth of the musical arrangements at that time, some of them having studied music formally. I was loved by her household.

Winston Soso my close friend also made a serious impact on Cubans with his smash hits, 'Big bottom', 'Panyard' and his songs were featured at every Caribbean party. I remembered telling the Cubans at one time that at the pace at which our music was progressing it was only a matter of time before a Vincentian artiste got a big break internationally and in the process, the world would get to know and love our music. Then Kevin Lyttle solidified my statement and hit the world charts with his smasher 'Turn me on'.

I would even venture to predict that in the next five years another Vincentian would take the world by storm and one of these artistes will do the trick:

1. Troots and Ice   2. Skarpyon   3. Winston Soso

4. Zolah   5. Squitty   6. Bomani

7. Problem Child   8. Danielle Veira   9. Madzart

10. Icon   11. Luta   12. Skinny Fabulous

13. Mystik Vibration   14. Jamesey P   15. Shanelle McKenzie

16. Tabia Matthews   17. Danielle Ollivierre   18. Gideon James

19. Gallanaire   20. Alston 'Becket' Cyrus   21. Lively

22. Abuza

This list is not etched in stone, it is subject to change and is based on the ability of the artistes to cross boundaries and experiment with different genres of music. I know Chavela would be excited when this happens. She would say, "That's music from Chester's country."

Chavela was one of Cuba's foremost neurosurgical nurses. She related some of the most complex surgeries in which she was able to assist the neurosurgeon while working at the institute. She was a very brilliant nurse and attained national success in neurophysiology and neuro-anatomy in yearly competitions held in Cuba for nurses. She won various scientific presentations in Cuba. I can always recall Chavela saying, "Chester your main role in life is to save lives and be of service to mankind and to help eradicate some of the medical problems in your country." I still cherish these words even as I write.

Carla

I met Carla in the early part of my specialization while attending a workshop on occupational safety. She was a mixture of white and mulatto. She was very beautiful with her hair flowing to her buttocks. Carla had delivered a paper on occupational safety on psychometrics.

I had a few questions to ask this psychologist. After a few minutes of conversation she asked, "Where are you from?" I replied quite frankly, "The Gem of the Antilles, the home of the blessed with no disrespect to Cuba, but the most beautiful country on earth." "Where is that?" she asked. And I replied, "St. Vincent and the Grenadines." She asked, "Is it the homeland of Theophilus Stevenson's father?" "You are so correct," I said. "I heard that your island is very beautiful, I have a friend who is coincidentally Manolo Ortegas' daughter who is married to a Vincentian, Donnie Defreitas. She lives there now." (Manolo Ortegas is Fidel Castro's former press Secretary). I then explained that I knew the couple and they were close friends of mine. "Small world isn't it?" she replied.

And it was so we became friends and started communicating by phone. One thing led to another, and we started dating. Carla was the cousin of Ricardo Alarcon a very high powered government official in the Cuban Communist party. When word leaked out that I was from St. Vincent and the Grenadines, she was summoned and was advised to dispose of me within 24 hours. She was cautioned by the military general that she was privy to many state secrets and it was not a wise idea for her to continue the relationship with a foreigner. Carla came to my home and broke the sad news to me. I was shocked and devastated and I must admit a little nervous. I felt as if I had committed an offence. She began to cry saying, "In my country, you are not even free to love." She had earlier revealed to me that she worked in a very sensitive military hospital having access to many classified state secrets and she knew before hand that she should not have entered into any relationship with a foreigner.

After this line of reasoning it was easier for me to accept that we should part especially when I realized that completing my medical studies was paramount. It was as though the saying that your happiness doesn't last very long was applicable in this relationship. It was Carla who had given me my first lesson in alternative medicine. She had a sound knowledge in herbology and had introduced me to Shiatsu massage. I remember her giving me bundles of dandelion, nettle, basil, rosemary and explaining the therapeutic value of each plant. She also introduced me to Edward Bach essences and floral therapy, a modality of treatment that I have worked with and from which I have derived tremendous results. I had treated her sister Fina who had fifteen years of infertility because of blocked fallopian tubes. She was ordered to undergo laparoscopic surgery which she simply refused. After treating her with Bach essences, within three months she became pregnant. Bach essences had worked wonders; of course I was the obstetrician/ Gynaecologist selected to assist in all antenatal checkups. Professor Nelson Rodriquez (world famous for Laparoscopic Surgery) and Professor Jose Oliva (world famous Ultrasonographer and Genetist) were my professors of inter-consultation. I also performed the c-section which resulted in a bouncing baby girl.

I understand that Carla no longer lives in Cuba. I can't wait for that day when we can speak again on friendly terms. I remember one of the humorous pieces she shared with me. A rat entered the central committee while a meeting was in progress. (The rat ran quickly across the room and one of Fidel Castro's ministers was sleeping in the meeting. He overheard various ministers in the meeting saying, "Catch him, catch him." To their amazement the minister awoke and shouted "and his brother also, and his brother also.") Immediately he was removed and charged for being a threat to national security. (It's a joke, no hard feelings Fidel)

Sandra

I met Sandra, a beautiful "darkie" from Mariañoa while pursuing the second year of my medical studies. Sandra was a beauty, Jennifer Lopez photocopied but a darker replica. I strolled into the University bookstore and I saw this African empress, her skin was black and shiny, and I reflected on the words of Solomon, "black and comely". I approached her and my heart was racing and at that moment I knew I had feelings for her.

I walked up to her and whispered softly, "You are the most beautiful lady I have seen in a very long time." She was astonished and somewhat surprised at my compliment, "Try a little harder," she said, "I almost fell for that line, tell me something I have never heard before." I began thinking quickly and responded spontaneously, "From the moment I saw you I understood perfectly that I knew not as yet what love is, it is so great the feeling that I'm willing to give you my heart and operate from batteries."

She blushed intensely and said, "I like that one, that's a first for me; I see that your Cuban friends have taught you a lot about persuading women. It's good to know you're not only learning about medicine here, but they were able to teach you other things." We became very good friends from that day onwards. She was extremely charming and intelligent with a strong religious background, and we enjoyed a very open relationship. She was a very unique person in my life in Cuba, as she assisted me in getting many of the reference books that were sometimes difficult to access. She had an interesting network to access medical information both electronically and otherwise. What was most interesting about her though, was that she assisted me many times when I was dead broke. She would make tasty dishes and bring them for me and all my friends while we studied into the wee hours of the morning.

Sandra and I spent wonderful moments in the company of each other.

Rosita

Rosita was a specially trained nurse in cancer management. She worked at the caner hospital in Havana. Her father was a top Cuban official in the ministry of health and her mother lived in Old Havana. It was there at her home that I got my second introduction to alternative medicine by her grandmother Lola. Rosita was tall, dark skinned with a broad smile. What was different about her smile though, was that when she smiled one could count thirty two teeth. Her teeth were very well aligned and she was very attractive resembling the famous Janet Jackson of Hollywood. I remember seeing her for the first time while visiting a friend of mine who was battling colon cancer. She had almost left the hospital and was approaching the area where bicycles were parked at that time. A friend of hers called, "Rosie, Rosie, I'll see you tomorrow." I walked right up to her and sang, "Rosie, Rosie I wanna be your honey." She smiled instantly and said, "You are out of place and rude at the same time." Noticing my accent she asked, "Where are you from?" I replied, "I am from the most romantic country in the world and I think you should spend the rest of your life with me there." She was surprised and said, "You must be a crazy man." She looked about twenty years old at that time. We enjoyed the joke together and after much persuasion over a period of weeks we began dating regularly. She spoke English fluently and we got along quite well. She was having a very hard time at home at that time and one day she eventually ran away from home to be with me; an act that I never approved of, but I could not persuade her to return. I could not accommodate her where I was living, so I had to rent a new house eventually. She was young, just turned nineteen and lacked experience. So I had to teach her a lot about life. Constantly I was being bombarded with threats from her mom about having my studies in Cuba terminated.

Rosita and I enjoyed many romantic outings, going to Tropicana night club, attending the theatre, dance, ballet and operas. Sometimes we spent long hours on the Cuban waterfront called Malecon. This was also called 'Lovers Lane' because of the hundreds of lovers that frequented this romantic spot almost nightly. It was Rosita who made me understand that Cuban Culture is a blend that goes beyond the ordinary. It is a hybrid of European and eastern culture, intertwined with Latin American and Caribbean cultural forms.

I got my first lesson in infidelity with Rosita when she 'hooked' up with a past boyfriend of hers after he won a medal at the Pan American games in Lucha Libre (wrestling). She abruptly ended the relationship saying that she was not sure she could live in a foreign country. I consoled myself with the thought that we were not meant to be. I was later evicted from the house I was renting which coincidentally was owned by her aunt. I was now poised to spend my worst day in Cuba.

My worst day in Cuba

It was September of 1995, I had just completed one of my most hectic 24 hours in a Cuban hospital. I was working in the delivery room of a Cuban Hospital   that day. We had about 75 deliveries during the 24 hours. I had completed about eight c-sections, one emergency hysterectomy, one extra-peritoneal c-section and a number of D and Cs on the gynaecological ward along with two ectopic pregnancies. We had a full night. As if this wasn't enough we had a number of patients being treated for preclampsia.

After I returned from the hospital to where I called home I met Rosie's aunt who said to me, "Rosie had informed me that you all are not together any more." I replied, "I haven't seen her for over a week now and she hasn't told me anything as yet." She replied, "Well I am telling you this. She doesn't want to be with you anymore, you are broke and she cannot be in love on a hungry belly. You owe me a month's rent and I don't want you living in my home anymore. Her new boyfriend has money and he travels a lot with the national sports team." I was shocked at what I was hearing. It made me realize that you never get to know people well until you see them when they are angry. We seldom had real heated arguments, everything just seemed to be okay, but her material needs were not being fulfilled with me. Her aunt thought I would have been closer to her because I was renting from her so she would have been able to capitalize on our friendship but this was not to be as I kept her at a distance at all times. She informed me that I had 24 hours to leave her premises, I told her twenty four was too much she should give me one hour. "I will pay you your rent money when I get back", I said as I was leaving to recover some monies that I had loaned to someone. I softly said to her, "The way you are treating me is unjust and all unfair games will be played again." Remembering a song from my good friend and calypsonian vibrating Scakes in his song, "Retribution coming if you cheat me and believe you win all unfair games will be played again." I have lived to see her aunt beg me for mercy and to forgive her for the unfair way she had treated me. But that's the nature of life in the real world; what's important though is that if you do any harm to anyone you should ask their forgiveness. I can't help but remember at this time a song mom used to sing called an unfinished task.

I left to recover the rent money and returned in a jiffy only to find my belongings on the porch. I felt like a worm that day. All of my neighbours were taking in the action. I heard one of my neighbours Pablo shout, "Doc doesn't deserve to be treated like a dog, he is a good man who saved many lives in this neighbourhood including some of your own relatives and mine." He was furious. 'Please, don't make me the cause of your next heart attack," she said alluding to the fact that Pablo had a heart attack sometime before and I was the one who had saved his life giving him CPR with mouth to mouth resuscitation. "He saved your life he hasn't saved mine yet." By this time all the neighbours joined with Pablo to show their disgust. Two other neighbours offered their homes to me free of cost until I had finished my studies or had found other accommodations. This was a very enticing offer bearing in mind my financial status at that time; but I was so ashamed of the dilemma that had just occurred that I couldn't accept the offer. "Stay here and we will take care of you doc," many of them shouted. I moved out all my personal belongings after I had paid her the rent and strolled out of the house trying to keep a straight face and an upright head. Shame was written all over my face, but I tried hard to contain it. I had two large suitcases and had left some of my books at Pablo's house. I had also treated Pablo's wife for infertility and she had succeeded in having a baby boy named Oscar (my godson). The neighbours shouted, 'Doc you are going because you want to, you can stay with us free of charge." I expressed my gratitude but at that moment I wished the earth could open so that I could disappear without them seeing me. I had to walk past all the persons and I still remember it as my most daring walk. I reflected that I had not suffered an ordeal like this, not even in my homeland where a prophet has no honour. It was my first encounter with public abuse by anyone. I reflected on how dangerous it is to be involved with persons who do not share your principles in life. It was what my mom used to call being unequally yoked. I also understood why persons in the central committee were not in favour of me living in that community. However I was able to see that there were persons who still cared genuinely and were willing to go above and beyond the call of duty to assist me in the worst time. It is only in conflict and contradiction where you see the best and worst in people.

As if that ordeal was not enough, I travelled to Reparto Monterrey where I sometimes spent a lot of time visiting my friend Luis Perez and his family. When I realized I was dying trying to pull these two suitcases, I decided to rest for a while. After resting for half an hour I continued on my pilgrimage until I reached the home where I was going. I met the owner of the house outside and to my surprise she didn't allow me to enter as she normally did. "What happen Chester Toney, where are you going with these two large suitcases?" I proceeded to explain what happened. She then replied, "I am so sorry I have some relatives visiting from Las Villas staying with me for the week, the house is full." I consoled her saying that I was okay. "I feel so sad to see you homeless," she replied. "Let me ask my neighbour to help you until tomorrow. I don't want you to be on the road so late especially with these two suitcases." "No, no, no, I said I'll find a place, don't worry." I set out once again on my journey to return to the place that I was running from. It was now around 11pm and I walked back to the park where I had just rested; to get my thoughts together and to wait on a bus to get back to town. I was dead tired and extremely hungry. I felt my intestines revolving inside of my abdomen inflicting excruciating pain on my exhausted frame. The noises from my intestines must have been audible even from a distance of three feet. I hoped that the people around were not listening. I had not eaten, not because of the lack of food, but because I had no appetite in the midst of all this dilemma.

In those days, the buses passed every two or three hours after midnight, so I knew I was doomed. I prepared myself mentally for a long haul. With my two suitcases as my bed and a bag of books as my pillow I relaxed after being so drained from the twenty four hour duty at the hospital and all that followed after. I must have slept from midnight to 5 a.m. before I was awakened by an elderly lady, "What a strong young man like you have here sleeping in a park with suitcases at that?" I told her that I had fallen asleep while waiting for a bus. "You a lucky man, last week a man was robbed here in this same park after he fell asleep while waiting on a bus." I felt chills running down my spine and all of the hair on my body stood up. I knew that night that the Lord had watched over me while I was asleep. "You are a foreigner, why are you sleeping here, why don't you go to your embassy?" she asked inquisitively. I once again related my plight and informed her that my country had no embassy in Cuba, and that I was practically on my own. She encouraged me to return to Havana and at that same moment the bus arrived. While on the bus I prayed to the Lord not to let me pass another day like this, at least not while I was in Cuba.

Why I became an Obstetrician/Gynaecologist

It is very common for a patient to ask me the question, "Doc why did you choose this field?" It's a question that always seems to have me thinking, but the bottom line remains the same. I became a Gynaecologist because of two main reasons. Firstly, I realized that I had great interest in the specialty, in that when I was not in deep studies, I was motivated to stroll into the Obstetrics and Gynaecology hospital in Vedado in Havana. I visited this hospital because here I had developed some of my deepest and most genuine friendships while in Cuba. On many occasions I visited just to say hello or as a means of distraction from my routine. Secondly, I excelled in the specialty and found myself lecturing students when they were in doubt about a particular topic pertaining to the specialty.

At first I wanted to become an orthopedic surgeon, but while rotating in this specialty as a medical student, I realized that it reminded me of carpentry. Though I had loved carpentry (woodworks) while at the Grammar School, I did not think it was easy to replicate my interest here on the human body. Maybe because the pins, screws, plates etc, just turned me off, when placed on the human body.

I was always sympathetic to the persons who had to have any of their extremities amputated. I believed in a conservative treatment which would run me into serious problems because I believe that amputation was the very last course of action to be taken when everything else had failed. So I know I had too many conflicts pursuing this specialty.

I found myself returning to the hospital with many patients and friends for medical attention and this happened more frequently in Obstetrics/ Gynaecology than in any other specialty. When I became an intern I was allowed to deliver many babies. I performed 123 deliveries as an intern in Obstetrics/Gynaecology. There was also a time when I was deeply passionate about plastic surgery and I performed a large number of operations assisted by a young surgeon named Beatriz. She taught me many techniques of breast reduction, tummy tuck, liposuction and transposition of the navel. I had a great time, it was really fun, and then it struck me that I would do very little work for the poor. Home in St. Vincent, there were not many persons willing or who could afford to do this type of surgery. I really wanted to work in a specialty where my knowledge of general medicine would still be of great use on a day to day basis. Being a plastic surgeon sounded quite 'romantic' but did not seem practical to me.

Then the deciding moment came. I was one of the most outstanding students in Gynaecology in my final exams. This then became the catalyst that propelled me into making my decision. And so it was, I decided to pursue a career in Obstetrics/Gynaecology. In Cuba it is considered to be one of the most overworked specialties. On the other hand I recognized that it was the only specialty in medicine where there is always excitement. The birth of a child is always an exciting moment except when there are problems. Hence, when you are on call, more often than not it is filled with excitement.

All of the midwives wanted me to start residency in Obstetrics/ Gynaecology. There was a unique case that occurred in the hospital where I worked. There was a patient whose name was Lazara who told the professor point blank, "I don't want you to touch me, the only person I want to touch me is Dr. Chester." (At that time I was still a medical student). The professor was highly annoyed and responded, "Look lady, I am not here to waste time, Dr. Chester is not a doctor as yet so you relax and let me examine you so I can leave here soon. I have a lecture to deliver and you are wasting my time." She did not budge, she went on the defensive and reiterated, "The only person that

I want to examine me gynaecologically is Dr. Chester. If you want you can supervise him, but he alone in here should examine me." The professor turned red like a tomato and said, "That's a lack of respect and I'm the one in charge here. Dr. Chester is just a medical student, it seems as though they brought you to the wrong hospital. In fact I better make arrangements for them to transfer you to the psychiatric hospital in central Havana or Masoro psychiatric hospital." She pulled herself together and begged the professor's pardon. He proceeded afterwards to examine her. I am told, that up to this day, this story is being told repeatedly in the hospital.

Personally, I am always considering the duty that was bestowed on a woman to carry and nurture the human species (from conception to death). Her main responsibility is to ensure that there is an environment of love. I once asked a professor of Obstetrics/Gynaecology what is his definition of a Gynaecologist. He looked at me as though he was surprised at the question and I could see him thinking deeply to give me an answer, and he replied, "You can read the definition of a Gynaecologist in any encyclopedia or dictionary, but the one I am going to give you, I want you to remember it until you die. He is a medical doctor who practises where people have fun." I found it very hilarious.

Chapter 12

Gracious deceit/generosity in reverse

I have encountered two classic cases of what I dub gracious deceit/ generosity in reverse. The first involves a medical student from another Caribbean island and the other case, I cannot comment much about because I believe the case will be going before the court. I am looking forward to giving you chapter and verse of this exciting debate between a 'friendemy' and myself. Don't miss this exciting drama.

I met Ernesto Solomon upon arrival from Camaguey to Havana. We were both from the Caribbean and we had something else in common; we were both medical students pursuing a career in Cuba under the same arduous circumstances. I clung to the phrase 'unity is strength'. I knew that I "would have his back" in confronting these trying circumstances.

At first Ernesto was very generous to me. He would go to the center of the city as we were living at La Victoria de Giron, the preclinical and basic medical sciences institute. Ernesto was 'God sent' to me, at least that's what I thought. Everything was going fine between us, but little did I know he was 'soft soaking' me for greater things.

One night, in the middle of my studies, Ernesto came to my room and interrupted me 'washing in tears'. He indicated that his father was very ill and he needed some money to travel back to his country (a Caribbean Island). I explained to him that my mom had sent me the money to purchase my ticket to return home after my first year of medicine. He assured me, swearing on his mom that he would return the money as soon as he got back. We counted simultaneously six hundred and fifty US dollars. "That's a loan," I cautioned him, "The only security I have is your word and our friendship, and to me a man is as good as his word." He was excited; the expression on his face was that of disbelief. "Chester, I'm so thankful that you can trust me, no one on this entire island would lend me this much, I'll always be grateful to you." And so he set off to see his ailing father. Later I was told that this was just a lie. He returned to Cuba and I was told that he did not travel to his homeland. I was very angry and disappointed at the extent to which I was taken for a ride by a son of the Caribbean and I spared no time in soliciting my money. He assured me that he would return my money before the semester was finished at the end of June. I eagerly awaited the return of my money at the end of the semester.

To my surprise Ernesto had left Cuba again, this time it was well known for the USA. I was furious. I had run out of every conceivable item - soap, food, detergent, toothpaste etc. I had no conceivable means of sustaining myself. I cried a river for the injustice that was dished out to me so blatantly by someone pretending to be my friend. I tried to escape my immediate realities, but the memories were too much. How could Ernesto treat me with such disdain? I couldn't contain the anger that was accumulating inside me. By the end of August Ernesto returned from the USA with two massive suitcases and immediately I went to his room to solicit my money once again. He was a black belt in karate and I had just been elevated to a brown belt in Judo. "Where's my money?" I asked him angrily. "I'll give you your money when I can!" he exclaimed, "And to make matters worse, if you come here to assault me I will not give you your money at all." At this moment my heart was racing with rage and I opted to be the aggressor contrary to what we were taught in Judo but was held back by two students from the Seychelles. It was a very unpleasant ordeal to see two Caribbean students almost physically fighting each other. It was then the words of Kenny Rogers came to my mind, "Son, you don't have to fight to be a man .... sometimes you gotta fight when you're a man." I was carried back to my room by the two students. "You are a thief, you are a thief," I shouted on my way back.

Ernesto had returned from the USA with a new look. He was dressed in the latest sneakers and wore some of the latest levi jeans at that time. He was ostentatious and spared no time flaunting his new "acquisitions" Meanwhile I continued with my scarcity but was given some assistance from two Jamaican friends, Colin Graham now Dr Colin Graham and Mark Sanderson now Dr Mark Sanderson.

After two weeks I received a communiqué to attend a meeting at the central committee building of the communist party of Cuba. Upon my arrival I met Ernesto, so I thought he had delivered my money to the party so I was somewhat excited. Little did I know that this was not to be. There was a gentleman who I knew very well who came to conduct the meeting with us in private; just the three of us. "I understand that you have tried to assault Mr. Solomon. But I want to inform you Mr. Toney that the communist party has no policy or dealings with students and US currency. We believe that the two of you should resolve this matter between both of you amicably. Now if we hear at anytime again that you two gentlemen were involved in any physical or verbal fight we will be terminating your studies and sending you back to your respective countries, and I mean it." I was surprised at the arrogant manner in which he had spoken to me and I could not help answering him. "This is not the right way to dispense justice. When the victim remains the victim then no justice had been served." He was taken aback at my response. "I saw you smiling with a quiet disposition but I never knew you were so insolent." "In St. Vincent, we say that I did not leave my mouth inside my mother. You are not accustomed to speaking to persons who respond to you, so when I speak to you, you feel intimidated," I continued, "I want it to be in the back of your mind until you die that I did not like how you treated this issue and it smells bad for your system." By this time Ernesto was saying to me, "Humble Chester, don't get yourself into any trouble now." I angrily replied, "You have already placed me in this situation, all I can tell you is, all unfair games will have to be played again."

I politely excused myself and left both of them in the room. On my way out I overheard Ernesto saying, "I brought you a pair of Nike sneakers and a tracksuit from the USA." "Thank you, when can you bring them for me?" he said. It was then I realized that my case was closed and I could only depend now on leaving him at Jesus's feet as my mom used to say.

I reminisced on all that had happened and it dawned on me that I had heard Ernesto boast one day, "I have many friends in high places". Up to this day he has never repaid me my money nor has he admitted owing me.

Unfortunately, this man is now a physician and a respectable citizen in his country. I still can't help saying that I have met some of the worst human beings (inhumane) in the corridors of a university. Lately I have been able to forgive him, consoling myself in the thought that maybe the harsh conditions under which we lived accelerated the possibility of seeing either the worst or best in a person and I was just unfortunate to have experienced the worst in flesh in the quest to survive. To such persons, good people are just stepping stones and generosity is interpreted as weakness. There's a Cuban saying that goes like this, "The strong live from the weak and the weak live from catching their royal". These human beings are generally good people as long as money is not involved in the relationship. They see life solely from a 'dollars and cents' point of view and this is sad for they would have missed so many things in life that don't cost money. I know you would venture to ask me if there is anything which does not cost money in this world, but if you think that everything in the world costs money then you haven't been in contact with the Father, the Son and the Holy Spirit. No wonder they say the best things in life are free. Deceit in whatever form and lack of generosity are never qualities an upright citizen should cultivate.

Chapter 13

Rare Cases of my medical practice from Cuba to St. Vincent

In my practice in Cuba and in St. Vincent, I have encountered some unique cases which I still remember vividly. I am humbled to have seen such rare cases; some of which you only read about in medical textbooks. I am about to reveal some very interesting cases which I have encountered as a medical doctor, some of which are worth a whole book.

Dextrocardia

It was July 1996; I was fresh out of medical school and pursuing a six months rotation in general surgery at Comondante Manuel Fajardo Hospital. This is part of the programme of residents in Obstetrics/ Gynaecology in Cuba. A gentleman of African descent walked into the hospital with a strange look on his face. He was sweating profusely and came straight to the surgical emergency room where a cardiologist or resident in cardiology is always stationed. He had his hand holding his chest as though complaining for pain. I tried to question him but he was signaling wait with the palm of his left hand. He was gasping for breath. I looked around and realized that there was no one accompanying him. I checked his pulse which was 120 beats per minute; his blood pressure reading was 150/90. All this time the gentleman did not utter a single word. I placed the stethoscope on his chest, and at that moment I realized something was wrong. I tried to obtain the apex beat and was unable to. At this moment I saw the gentleman smiling and he pointed to the other side of his chest. I was a little perplexed but I proceeded to check the other side of his chest and bingo! I realized that the heart was located on the right and not on the left side of his chest. The left side is what is considered to be anatomically normal.

By this time he had relaxed and his clinical symptoms of ill health had subsided. "Don't be scared, my heart is on the right side and at times I get these episodes of the sensation of the heart racing fast. The doctors call this Tachycardia. This is generally accompanied by shortness of breath, but I feel much better now." I replied, "My, my, my, I have never seen a patient like this before." "This is called Dextrocardia," he interrupted, "And most doctors anywhere in the world do not see this condition regularly." At this time the cardiologist on call had approached us to find out what was wrong. I then referred the patient to the cardiologist for continuous supervision and also a more in depth diagnosis. I understood later that he was having some domestic stress which was having serious psychosomatic manifestations. The cardiologist assured me that he would have been alright and that he had placed him under a new regimen of medications. I never saw him again.

Supernumerary breast

In 2003 a young lady about eighteen years old visited my clinic complaining of severe headaches. I asked the pertinent questions to complete her clinical history and proceeded to have an examination done. While performing the examination I noticed that she was hiding her armpits and to my surprise she turned her face sideways awaiting a reaction. Close examination revealed a Supernumerary breast, a complete breast with a nipple to complete it. Supernumerary breast is a condition where the migration of breast tissue to the appropriate region was incomplete in the embryological development where breast tissue remains in the axillar region in this case. I consulted her and assured her that it was nothing to be ashamed of and that I could assist her in surgically removing the breast. She was then referred to a general surgeon to have the breast removed.

Aplastic Anemia

This is a medical condition characterized by a deficient red blood cell production and a disorder of the bone marrow. It is considered to be fatal. It is very rare in the Americas and Europe and occurs in one in every million persons. In Asia it's a little more prevalent. Chloramphenicol is a known drug that can cause this condition and more so in the oral form of the drug (tablets). In Cuba in Manuel Fajardo Hospital I had the privilege of seeing such a case. We know that Chloramphenicol is used widely as eye/ear drops. In 1991 I was able to see a forty year old man of Indian descent succumb to this disease and the only information collected of him having exposure to this drug was the use of an eye drop which he said he used anytime he had an infection of the eyes. This case has changed the course of my medical practice up to this day for I have never prescribed this drug.

Acrania

In 1997 during my practice in Havana a twenty six year old female twenty weeks pregnant attended my antenatal clinic at Ramon Gongalez Corro Hospital. She stated that she had been unable to sleep for weeks due to rapid fetal movements. After examination I proceeded to have an ultrasound done. To my surprise the demarcation of the cranium was absent. The image on the ultrasound looked rather unusual. There were undulating lines not considered to be the normal ultrasonographic impression of the craneo of the fetus. The bones of the skull of the fetus were absent. This is called acrania. This is a condition that is unsuitable to sustain life. She was admitted to the hospital and an interruption of the pregnancy was performed and genetic tests were done on the fetus and parents after the interruption. She was also scheduled for continuous counseling.

Agensia of the vagina

A young lady from a rural village visited my clinic sometime in April of 2005. She was eighteen years old and had never menstruated in her entire life. After a close examination, a fused vagina was seen with a minute opening. She related that she had tried to have sex on different occasions but was unsuccessful as penetration was impossible. I explained to her that she would have to undergo reconstructive surgery and this is generally done by a multi-disciplinary team of a general surgeon, an urologist and a gynaecologist. Sometimes a very skilled surgeon or gynaecologist will be able to perform the operation by himself. I have seen only one case of this type of surgery in my lifetime.

Collapse of the umbilical cord

It was 1993 in Havana City. 'Special period' was taking a toll on the face of the average Cuban. This was a period of real hardship and sacrifice and no one knew how long these arduous economic conditions would last. Cuba was no longer the recipient of aid and trade from the Eastern block of European countries, and so eighty percent of aid was truncated. It was the Souviet Union where military assistance, trade, technical support, in synthesis almost everything came from. Can you imagine what would happen if in your country 80 percent of trade and investment were to evaporate overnight? Only Cuba could have survived such an ordeal. More so, they survived without having civil unrest or civil disobedience. They were able to reconstruct their economy on the heels of so many natural disasters annually and still provide for their people, with many social services at an affordable cost. The economic situation in Cuba was at an all time low at that time, everything was scarce or non-existent. Most Cubans were sandwiched between a rock and a hard place. The majority of foreign students studying in Cuba at that time were uncertain if they would ever finish their studies. The shops were empty. The lines grew longer to purchase food and other items, and the ration cards for state assistance were the order of the day. Fidel Castro boldly proclaimed in the midst of this unpleasant scenario, "I will not let a single Cuban go hungry; we will not send home a single foreign student even though our students are being sent home by the hundreds by the governments in Eastern Europe. We will turn to alternative sources of living and in many years to come many countries will be jealous of Cuba for we will have one of the healthiest populations on earth. We will turn to bicycles, thus lowering environmental pollution and decreasing the levels of obesity. We will make a new Cuba that the world will envy. You would not see it now but the harvest will come in the future." I was moved by his vision and his charisma and every Cuban felt the sacrifices they were making now would pay great dividends in the future.

Cubans flocked to the popular uptown restaurant and fast food outlet 'Pio Pio' to purchase fried chicken and French fries. Many Cubans were frustrated and periodically you would hear sarcastic remarks like, Long live the revolution; socialism or death; capitalism is bad; free market enterprises are inhumane; Capitalism is exploitation of man by man. The restaurant was packed like sardines in a tin with locals and foreign students alike, all eager to source their meals for that day and many days to come. The restaurant was hot like a furnace, and then a pregnant lady fainted. An elderly woman rushed to her assistance and exclaimed in a loud voice, "She's bleeding, she's bleeding. Is there a doctor around?" I was accompanied by a classmate Eduardo Tamayo. We looked at each other almost instinctively and immediately eased our way through the crowd to the scene. "Excuse us; excuse us we are medical students,' we shouted. We took control of the scene immediately and asked the crowd to retreat from her. She was unconscious and I began to initiate CPR. She regained partial consciousness instantly, and it was at this time I realized that the bleeding was from her underwear accompanied by a collapsed umbilical cord. I was conscious at this time that time was of the essence here. It was imperative that we save both the life of the fetus and that of the mother at all cost. We flagged down a vehicle and wasted no time in getting her into it. I took off my T-shirt and began to dry up the blood from the car seat; she was bleeding profusely. I realized that she had drifted out of consciousness again, so I instructed Tamayo to continue CPR. At this time I pushed my hands into the birth canal to arrest any compression of the umbilical cord by the head of the fetus, thus allowing the fetus continuous oxygenation. Though I was cognizant of the dangers of HIV infection, I could not resist coming to her assistance. Logically we had no gloves to cover our hands; but of course HIV/AIDS was not so popular on the streets because persons who were infected were placed in a sanatorium (quarantine), and I knew from experience gained working at the hospital that all pregnant ladies were obligated to undergo complete antenatal tests. We approached Hospital Americarias (Maternidad de linea) and rushed her to the accident and emergency ward for assistance. The doctors on call welcomed our initiative and took responsibility of the emergency. A resident took over from me by placing his hands with gloves in the birth canal to arrest the compression of the umbilical cord on the head of the fetus. She was rushed to the operating theatre where later a c-section was performed. Two lives were saved by our decisive actions and this is a measure of satisfaction one derives from being a doctor. As a mark of gratitude, the mother named the baby Chester-Eduardo. It's amazing the number of mothers who have named their babies after me in Cuba. You will be surprised to know the number of Chesters or Toneys there are in Havana.

Burch Procedure by Laparascopy

History was made in the Republic of Cuba in 1997. Seven doctors set out on a mission to perform the world's first ever Burch Procedure by Laparascopy. This means in medical terms to correct urinary incontinence using Burch Procedure, but done by Laparascopy. Burch Procedure is an operation done frequently by the gynaecologist or urologist in which a sling is sutured to or around the neck of the bladder to the iliopectineal ligament. It is used to alleviate stress incontinence in women. It is not the only procedure but it is very effective.

Ramon Gonzales Corro Hospital is a top hospital in Cuba specializing in Obstetrics and Gyneacology/sexology. This prestigious medical institution is the center of reference nationally for Obstetrics, Gyneacology and sexology in Cuba. It is also a center of reference of sexology in Latin America. The medical team included Cuba's top Laparoscopic surgeon professor Nelson Rodriquez, Doctor Luis Forte, Dr Rafael Ramirez, a Columbian resident in Obstetrics/Gyneacology, Dr Sergio Parejas, Dr Alberto Martinez, Dr Humberto Arcos, Dr Jesus Valdes and yours truly resident Chester Toney of St. Vincent and the Grenadines. The preparations for this operation were meticulously done, first by an exhaustive selection of the case three months prior to the surgery. Each physician on the medical team had a specific task to perform prior, during and after the operation. We operated laboriously for over two and a half hours in the operating theatre with much progress. The whole operation was captured on video. Just when we were about to create history in medical science a mishap took place. There were some anesthetic complications and we had to revert to the original Burch Procedure to minimize the patients anesthetic time. We were disappointed at the final stage. We had to abort our stalwart efforts. We remained resolute that we would complete the mission one day. It would have been tragic to continue and we were determined to make history record us as caring for the patient's life and not a bunch of doctors trying to create history at the cost of someone else's life. Our valiant effort will always be remembered at Ramon Gonzales Corro Obstetrics and sexology hospital. However, there were several lessons learnt from our noble cause. One of these lessons is that one can never predict with certainty how a patient would react under the influence of an anesthetic, neither can one underestimate the role that anesthetics play in the success of any operation no matter how simple the operation may be.

This International team of doctors was united in purpose and action. We learnt how simple and humble doctors were world class in their own right in complicated surgical procedures. The anesthesiologist during the operation was Dr Julio Delfin Villa.

Unique case of low sperm count

Infertility is defined as the inability to achieve conception after one year of unprotected intercourse between two adult persons biologically male and female at birth. Generally they should be living under the same roof. A woman who habitually miscarries or continually delivers so early that she's unable to carry full term a mature fetus capable of surviving is also considered to have infertility problems.

On a Friday of March 2004 a young lady and her husband walked into my clinic, both of them with tears streaming down their faces, relating that they had just visited their doctor who had been treating them for infertility for the past one and a half years, and that he was unsuccessful. She alluded to the fact that her husband was diagnosed with a low sperm count, only ½ million/volume initially, and after a year and a half of treatment it had jumped 1 million/volume. She was quick to refer to what the previous doctor had advised her. "Adopt a child or save your money to pursue in-vitro fertilization". By this time, her husband was crying, "He made me feel less of a man" he said. I counseled them assuring him that he was no less of a man and with his persistence and compliance with what I was about to prescribe and advise, they both will be happy in the end, 'I'll do anything that you advise me to and take any medication that you prescribe," he said full of optimism. I wasted no time. I began revising copies of complimentary tests he had done over the past year and a half, including three spermmogrammes. I proceeded to a new course of treatment comprising firstly, colon cleansing, chiropractic adjustments, mineral and vitamin therapy, dieting and fasting, herbology and juice therapy along with certain techniques for fertility that can be used during intercourse.

After six months the spermmogramme revealed that it was now 15 million/volume and the motility (movements) of the cells was 40 percent compared to 10 percent previously. I then complemented the treatment with conventional drugs after six months to assist in his condition. After nine months of treatment his wife became pregnant and delivered a beautiful bouncing baby girl.

Extraction of a third molar under acupuncture

I did not include this in the above mentioned rare experiences in medicine in an extensive manner because of specific reasons. However, I will elaborate in another publication soon.

These experiences that I've gained in my medical practice over the years have shown me that everyone is in fact created differently and that doctors can never have total control over life and knowledge of life. These cases were meticulously selected also to be used as a guide for persons with non-medical training to get a glimpse of the physician on a day to day basis on how he confronts complex situations. I hope that you have found these cases very interesting and they have contributed to your wealth of knowledge in the medical profession.

Happy Reading!

Chapter 14

Encounter with Dr. Chester Toney, interviewed by Neville Thompson, freelance journalist at Indian bay, a panoramic view of the Grenadine islands in the background.

Journalist: Good afternoon (Shaking hands with the doctor, sitting on a chair facing Young Island as he starts recording)

Dr. Toney: Good afternoon Neville (smiling with back turned to the Grenadine Islands)

Journalist: How are you today doc? Let's see if I can remember how you say that in Spanish. Bueñas tardes doctor? ¿cómo estás? No ¿cómo está?

Dr. Toney: (Chuckling) Very good Neville, very good. I'll try to respond to you in Spanish as you asked. Bueñas tardes Neville estoy muy bien gracias. I see you have remembered quite a bit of Spanish, your Spanish teacher would be quite proud of you. At least you didn't disappoint her.

Journalist: (Chuckling) Thank you doc. How has your day been so far, have you been busy?

Dr. Toney: Yes, I've been extremely busy; you know the life of a medical doctor, managing family commitments and medical obligations at the same time. A doctor generally has to divide him/herself into two or more different entities to fulfill each party's desire at the same time. Look today, I dropped Jennifer and the children off at the beach and I could only spend one hour playing with them, as I had three patients who called needing medical attention. I had to end my playing time with the boys abruptly to hurry back to the office to be of service. Sometimes I have to make great sacrifices; just like now I could have been playing with them over there, but I have to get this long overdue interview done for inclusion in my book 'The unapologetic quest for success'.

Journalist: (Sipping on a Hairoun beer, national beer of St. Vincent and the Grenadines) Well let's get started (putting his beer on the table) How long have you spent studying in Cuba?

Dr. Toney: I spent eleven years studying in Cuba. It's rather coincidental, I left St. Vincent on 17th September 1987 and returned on 17th September 1998, you see.........

Journalist (interrupts): Excuse me Dr. Toney, are you the Vincentian who studied the longest there? You almost didn't come back home.

Dr. Toney: I'm not too sure; I think I'm in that category of students who stayed the longest there. In my case, I specialized in Obstetrics and Gynaecology and post graduate diplomas relating to alternative medicine. It's amazing how my image of the world changed over those years. I set out on a mission in the late 1980's when students had to hide to go to Cuba. One couldn't disclose to certain persons for fear of being sabotaged or obstructed from leaving. Nevertheless, it was Cuba that resurfaced the noble concept of Christianity which I learnt, love thy neighbours as thyself. It amplified that philosophy of egalitarianism. I also realized that in Cuba the world was in fact a small place. Havana is a cosmopolitan city in which persons from all over the world converge to study and everybody speaks Spanish to communicate. It was so easy for me to speak to someone from Laos, Cambodia, Ivory Coast, Benin, Mongolia, Seychelles, Burundi, Sudan and Chad, countries you generally do not hear about regularly. It was common for students to have heated discussions about sports, music and current affairs. Havana is truly a melting pot of many cultures, races and religions. What is significant though, is that nearly eighty percent of the students studying there were originally from humble beginnings and they had to grasp the opportunity to lift themselves up by their own bootstraps. It was in Havana that I came close to many who had fought wars in their homelands, and I was given a first hand description about the effects of war. I was impressed by some of these students (especially those from Angola), their appreciation of 'life' and 'peace'.

Journalist: Do you have any regrets about going to Cuba, and if so, would you do it all over again?

Dr. Toney: That's a brilliant question Neville. Let me start like Frank Sinatra: "Regrets, I have a few but too few to mention"; or something like that.

Dr. Toney and Neville laughing simultaneously.

Dr. Toney: Ok on a serious note Neville, I have few regrets about going to Cuba to study and I will not do it differently if I were to go again. I must state categorically that Cuba gave me a greater vision and mission about life in general. I see life from a less material point of view. Frankly, my sojourn to Cuba resonates a lot with the title of the book, "The unapologetic quest for success." I make no apologies for trying to succeed in whatever I do. Cuba opened my eyes to pursue unending wisdom, knowledge and understanding. It gave me an insatiable thirst to serve humanity.

It was ridiculous upon my return from Cuba after eleven years, with a medical degree of a specialist Obstetrician /Gynecologist and many other post graduate diplomas that the status quo wanted to make me feel that I made the wrong choice in going to Cuba. It is amazing that some of these same persons, who fought against me getting a job, now have sons and daughters studying in Cuba. How ironic! Some of them are so guilty of the injustice perpetrated against me at that time, that up to today they cannot look me straight in the eyes. I hold no malice, one should not fill one's heart with such negative emotions. My mom used to say that bitterness is a cup of poison that you drink yourself hoping that the other person will be ill in the process.

So I believe that the year after I returned from Cuba was the most difficult year of my entire life, not working, trying to get a job and at the same time build a clinic. This year was worse than the eleven years of "special period" in Cuba. I endured more hardship from my own people, but I got solace from the Bible. A prophet has no honour in his homeland. I persevered untiringly in my quest to succeed, I remain unapologetic up to this day. You see Neville, when one tries to belittle the blessings of someone on whom the Lord has bestowed that blessing, He takes a portion of the blessing that He had for that person and gives it to you.

Journalist: What are your impressions of Cuba after eleven years living there?

Dr. Toney: (Drinking 'Mountain top' spring water) Excuse me please Neville, (putting down the glass) I think I remember Cuba as a place where I felt loved. I walked down the streets of Havana, and I was greeted by so many persons, it was unbelievable. The Cubans made me feel that I was a special person whom they grew to love as a 'brother'. Interestingly though, my love for St. Vincent and the Grenadines became more abundant in Cuba. Many persons who knew me well will comment on the presence of the large Vincentian flag in my room wherever I moved to in Cuba while there. Cubans are people who are satisfied with very little, they are hardworking and very generous to others who are less fortunate.

Every time I remember the supreme sacrifices that they make and their level of generosity, my respect and love for them grow stronger. I remember just as though it was yesterday when I was leaving Cuba. I gave away all my material possessions that I had accumulated over the last eleven years, from home stereo system, clothes and appliances to a very dear gold citizen watch.

You know, when I was leaving José Martí international airport, a friend that I gave my citizen watch saw me without a watch and said, "Chester, you can't go back to St. Vincent a big Gynaecologist and you are not even wearing a watch, come on man, they will think that you are lying." So I replied, "You know, I don't bother myself about material things." And so he took off the Russian made watch that he was wearing and placed it on my hand. Tears almost came to my eyes. Up to this day I cherish this watch with all my heart.

Journalist: What were the changes that confronted you as a new Gynaecologist upon opening your clinic?

Dr. Toney: I had the shock of my life upon opening my clinic after one year of seeking employment. This was my second major lesson in capitalism and how it works.

You see after spending most of my adult life in a socialist country, at that time I was not so much exposed to private medical practice. I was struggling to make ends meet, patients were very few, sometimes one per day, and sometimes no one showed up. I held my own even though the small town propaganda was prominent and vicious. There was a rumor circulating that there was uncertainty about my credentials and experience. God knows how much I struggled at that point. I had owed ten months rent. Thanks to Mr. Vivian Bonadie (deceased) and family I was given a grace period to pay (which I eventually did). I had to improvise to survive. Sometimes I would remember some of the lucrative contracts I had turned down from South Africa, Spain and Brazil to be in my homeland. I felt defeated, rejected, abused, misused, refused and confused. It was very hard. I would cry at times and my mom would say, "You have done the right thing my son, we are in this together, I am glad you are here with me and that's what matters most." She would also say, "God has greater plans for you, that's why he's hardening you like this. He has a greater calling for you, he is only testing your faith." I prayed night and day for him to vindicate me, and that my practice would grow from strength to strength, and that one day I would be known all over the world. That day is yet to come. My day is yet to come, to God be the Glory! I still have many short-comings and challenges but they are not as harsh and unbearable as when I first started.

Journalist: What's your clientele like at the clinic and what services do you provide?

Dr. Toney: A wide cross section of the population attends my clinic. Persons from some of the neighbouring Caribbean islands including Barbados, Carriacou, Grenada, and St. Lucia. We provide services at Lifeline Medical Clinic in Gynaecology, Obstetrics, Sexology and Alternative Medicine. One thing I can guarantee any patient coming to my clinic, is that there is no prejudice nor discrimination, and all patients are treated with love, respect, empathy and care. We may not be perfect, but the services we provide are excellent. In fact, our visions is: "The doctor of the future will give no medicine but will interest his patients in the care of the human frame in diet and the cause and prevention of disease."(Thomas Edison) We believe that the role of a doctor is to help preserve life. A doctor cannot prevent death from occurring, but he can treat you to improve and prolong your life.

Journalist: It is said that you refused to work at the hospital, in fact it is said they gave you a job.

Dr. Toney: No, that's ridiculous. I was never given a job. A proposal was made to me to be DMO (District Medical Officer) attached to the then Kingstown General Hospital. They outlined that there was no vacancy and one had to be reasonable within the circumstances. Taking a job like this would have been historic; it would have been the first time that a Gynaecologist took up such a junior post. Also remember that I had borrowed to self finance my studies overseas. The salary, working conditions, job description and other arrangements turned me off from accepting such a proposal. At the same time they were trying to prevent me from registering as a doctor in the state of St. Vincent and the Grenadines. They all know who they were, they practically ganged up against me, it was inhumane to say the least. I cried day and night for the injustice they were perpetuating against me. God is good, I forgive them, for their blessings would become mine. I've never stopped reading my Psalms from that day onwards, some of them I can recite word for word including Psalms 17.

Journalist: Are you following the changes unfolding in Cuba today, and if so what are your opinions?

Dr. Toney: Yes, I've been following the changes occurring in Cuba via telephone conversations with close friends whom I still chat with on a regular basis. The changes taking place in Cuba are inevitable. I applaud the partial opening up of the telecommunication sector to allow Cubans to own cell phones and computers, and also some leniency in ownership of businesses in the private sector. There have to be modifications in the modus operandi. What I'm concerned about though is, does Raul Castro have the cohesive ingredient to keep Cuba together if he opens up the country to other new changes that occur from the effects of globalization, trade liberalization and information technology. Let's be frank, Cuba has to change as the whole world is changing. I know Fidel Castro fought tirelessly against many western influences such as homosexuality rights, same sex marriages and legalization of the prostitution act.

Journalist: What advice would you like to give to Raul Castro about the governance of Cuba and the new American president who took office in January?

Dr. Toney: If I were to give any advice to Raul Castro and the new U.S. president about the governance of Cuba, I would say that Mr. Castro should encourage more frank discussions with Washington about the future of the island. It doesn't mean dismantling the system but modifying it to some extent so that there could be more meaningful and productive interchange between them. To the new president Barack Obama, the US embargo is forty seven years old and has proven to be a failure in toppling the Government.

Barack Obama must be congratulated for lifting travel restrictions for Cuban families both in the U.S.A and Cuba. He should also be commended for abolishing restrictions placed by the George Bush administration on remittances to Cuba from the USA. Come on, come on, both parties need to think of their people first instead of their own political agenda. America you say you are the dean of human rights, so lead by example. It would be interesting to see how Raul Castro handles these new changes, remember one hand cannot clap. The USA also needs to start the ball rolling in dismantling this oppressive embargo that has been a failure for nearly fifty years.

Journalist: How do you see Raul Castro as the new leader of Cuba?

Dr. Toney: Raul Castro has recently allowed U.N representatives to inspect his notorious prisons, advance the issue of freedom of expression and human rights. Fidel had serious reservations about doing so. Some think that Raul has a mind of his own and is willing to break away from the image of his elder brother Fidel, and by extension breaking family traditions (Fidel had surrendered power to his brother in 2006).

Journalist: Fidel is eighty three years old today Raul is seventy seven years old. How do you see Fidel Castro's leadership over the past forty-six years?

Dr. Toney: Many persons who never lived in Cuba wonder how one man could govern a country so long. What they fail to understand is that the Cuban revolution was not impressed on its people. It was created out of the people and led by Fidel Castro, Ernesto Che Gueverra and Cuban revolutionaries. Revolutionaries are born out of subjective and objective conditions in any country at a particular time in that country's history. Of course the objective conditions always exist. One has to give Fidel Castro some credit for staying in power so long for there was never a person who was able to take power away from him during his tenure of leadership. He has outlived nine United States Presidents and four decades of economic embargo against Cuba. Fidel can boast that he has made significant changes in education, health, science, sports, culture and other areas. In fact Cuba can boast of being first in some of the aforementioned disciplines. Some argue that he lived a life above the average Cuban, but he has much to show to the world. He has transformed Cuba and its human resources in a tangible manner. Fidel has been intransigent and non-compromising with the U.S. Sometimes I personally did not agree with his positions, but that's the nature of the man, he has a mind of his own; and in the long run he is the leader.

Journalist: How do you see the relationship between Cuba and the U.S.A in the future now that Fidel is not the leader?

Dr. Toney: Both Cuba and the U.S.A need to sit down and straighten out their differences and arrive at a civil and peaceful agreement. Cuba is much greater than Fidel Castro or Raul. America is not Obama.

There are much greater historical links between both nations and they have to adjust some of their positions and differences on each side of the bargaining table. I personally would like to see Cuba as a socialist country adopting some of the economic measures of the People's Republic of China whereby there is greater openness towards capitalism by establishing a special economic zone such as what we have seen unfolding before our eyes there. The Chinese have been able to attract foreign investors which have resulted in the alleviation of poverty of hundreds of millions ordinary Chinese citizens in the last twenty years. Cuba will thrive well on a similar arrangement bearing in mind they have many well-trained professionals and technicians. I will also like to see Cubans having the right to travel, trade and own properties etc. I know I have opened a can of worms here because of my close association with many members of the revolution, but freedom of choice should be the right of every human being. We have to respect people's choices even though we don't agree with them.

It is generally said that a nation gets the government it deserves. In essence, the people decide who they want to govern them and what direction they should pursue.

Journalist: Do you have any special words you'd like to say to him?

Dr. Toney: Yes Neville, I'd be glad to take this opportunity to extend to you Fidel, happy 84th birthday in advance. I read your speeches a lot while in Cuba and stood up once in revolution square and listened to you for four hours. You are one of the world leaders whom I really love and respect. Mandela is my first love. Please don't get jealous and I'll tell you why. Mandela is the only world leader to date who brought tears to my eyes. You are next in line followed by

J.F.K and Obama. I would like to thank you Fidel from the bottom of my heart for assisting me in becoming a doctor.

Thanks also to my Cuban professors, but above all, to God be the glory. Fidel I'm grateful for your assistance and your generosity. You are the man! I would also like to state on behalf of all Vincentians who have studied there and by extension all Caribbean students. Your name would be in our hearts and our children's hearts long after you are gone. I will remember you as a champion of the poor, oppressed and the discriminated. I will remember your contribution in saving Africa from apartheid. As my mom taught me, ingratitude is worse than witchcraft.

Journalist: Are you in contact with regular Cuban citizens after returning from Cuba on an ongoing basis?

Dr. Toney: Yes, I can't forget my friends; I have many whom I communicate with regularly. I still give generously to many of my close friends who assisted me over the years. Some have helped me as a student, others in my four years of residency of Obstetrics and Gynaecology there. I've sent remittances back to close friends and associates from time to time. There's a Cuban saying, 'Never look to whom you're doing good.' I can never be ungrateful to the Cuban people, never! I may share a different ideology, but that should not hinder us from cooperating and bringing good to humanity, so that we can live together peacefully.

Journalist: Cuba has trained over two hundred and fifty Vincentian nationals. There are more than two hundred more studying now at various universities. They are one of the major players in the construction of the Argyle International Airport with technical assistance in various aspects of the country's economy. How do you evaluate the assistant given to St. Vincent by the Cubans?

Dr. Toney: I say great Neville. Cuba is a country with scarce resources and is helping more than many countries that have so much wealth. You will recall that they were also assisting in the construction of the Point Salines International Airport in Grenada now renamed the Maurice Bishop International Airport, when Grenada was invaded by the U. S in 1983, and the Cubans working there lost their lives trying to defend the airport. Although I have my personal reservations about the composition of the other countries helping to construct our airport, I salute the efforts, for at times it is not who you want to help in your time of need, but who is willing to help you. As a layman on airport construction, (I may be corrected if I'm wrong and if I'm wrong I apologize) but I believe there should have been more detailed studies done on the prefeasibility of the airport and the airport site selection, and a well detailed environmental impact assessment done over a longer period of time. I also would have liked to know that the wind studies would have been completed before construction of the airport even began (common sense was made before book) and that the future stakeholders would have been more actively involved in the development process.

Nevertheless, it is a brave and creative venture and is highly commendable, and the government along with the 'coalition of the willing' must be commended for its vision (where there's no vision the people perish). There is reason though for some cautious hope about the date of completion of the airport, bearing in mind what is happening globally with respect to the economic meltdown. But I will be glad to see that it is finished within the stipulated time.

Journalist: How do you see yourself in the next ten years, God's willing?

Dr. Toney: I see myself in the next ten years as an objective thinking Vincentian (an independent), not beholding to nor financed by any political machinery. I see myself not operating in a dogmatic manner to any political party whether locally, regionally or internationally.

I have some very big dreams that I would like to pursue for St. Vincent and the Grenadines and by extension myself. We must teach our children the virtues of tilling the soil and planting the seeds. We must teach them about the importance of service especially to the community transferring dialectally the existing realities of the island, cognizant of globalization, trade liberalization and information technology. Our education system needs to be revamped, it needs to be less static. My big dream though, is to complete four major projects. Firstly, the establishment of an ethno-botanic institute to develop indigenous pharmaceuticals here in St. Vincent and the Grenadines.

Secondly, the establishment of a reproductive science institute that deals specifically with assisted fertilization/invitro-fertilization) also, to provide health tourism services on par with any country in the world in various alternative medicine disciplines. And, to construct a wax museum similar to that at Madame Tussaud in London (which I visited in 2002) to showcase our Vincentian and Caribbean greats who I would propose as the following:

Maurice King	Former Pan-American games silver medalist in weight lifting (light weight) in 1959and was ranked number 2 in the world.
Elsworth "Shake" Keane	He was ranked as one of the world's greatest flugel horn players in the 1950s and 1960s. (Some argue that he was the greatest). Shake Keane was also called one of the most innovative fathers of modern Caribbean literature by admirers like George Lamming. He has won many International poetry awards including Cuba's Premio Casa De Las Americas 1979 Poetry Literary Prize with his winning collection "One a Week With Water'.
Hugh Mulzac	He became the first black man to become a sea captain of a US Merchant Marine Fleet. It is widely believed that his colour of skin was used to deny him the opportunity to command the ship during the Second World War, although he was already a qualified captain for over twenty years. He was finally given his command after the completion of the war when he shipped as Master of the Booker T. Washington in 1947. He was the first coloured officer to be given the distinction in the United States navy.

Kevin Lyttle	World famous for his smash hit "Turn me on".

Earl 'Ole George' Daniel and Joel Butcher

World record in endurance walking, having broken the world record four times previously. They walked eight days without sleep in Central Park, USA.

Alston 'Becket" Cyrus	World famous for his international hit 'Teaser". In 1994 Becket received BMI Latin award for Ella me Vacila/Esa Chica.
Winston Soso	The Rolls Royce of calypso, famous for his hit song "I don't mind".
Adonal Foyle	NBA basket ball star
Sancho Lyttle	WNBA star
Sophia Young	WNBA star
Theophilus Stephenson	Three times Olympic gold medalist in heavy weight boxing, representing Cuba. His father was a Vincentian and was bestowed "honorary" citizenship when he visited St. Vincent in the 1980s to see his relatives.
Joseph Chatoyer	Paramount Chief of the Black Caribs. Our only National Hero of St. Vincent and the Grenadines so far.
Winston Davis	He was part of the West Indies 1983 world cup cricket squad. He set a world record (at that time) of seven wickets for 51 runs against Australia in Headingley.

Frankie McIntosh	Arguably the finest arranger of calypso music who ever lived.

I would also like to include other persons from other Caribbean countries like:

Trinidad:

Brian Charles Lara	The highest first class individual score 501 not out and the highest test score 400 not out in cricket.

Penny Commissiong   Former Miss Universe.

Otto Boldon   Former 200 metre world championship.

Hazley Crawford	100 metre gold medalist in 1976 Montreal Olympics
V.S Naipaul	Nobel Prize winner in literature
Winston 'Spree' Simon	The man who invented the steel pan, some argue he was born in SVG.

The Mighty Sparrow Slinger Francisco Born in Grenada calypso King of the world.

Grenada:

Maurice Bishop	Revolutionary and visionary leader.

St. Lucia:

Sir Arthur Lewis	Nobel Prize Winner in economics.
Derek Walcott	Nobel Prize Winner in Literature.

Dominica:

Dame Eugina Charles	One of the first female Prime Ministers in the world.

Antigua and Barbuda:

Sir. Vivian Richards	Rated to be among the five (5) most prolific cricketers who ever played the game in the 20th century.

Sir. Vivian Richards — Rated to be among the five (5) most prolific cricketers who ever played the game in the 20th century.

Curtley Ambrose — One of the greatest fast bowlers who played the game of test cricket. He has over 400 test wickets.

St. Kitts/Nevis:

Kim Collins — Former commonwealth and world championship gold medalist in 100 metres.

Monsterrat:

'The Mighty Arrow' Fonsie Cassel, Famous for his hit song 'Hot Hot Hot'

Jamaica:

Bob Marley — Considered to be the most influential singer of the second half of the 20th century.

Marcus Garvey — Pan African Activist, creator of the back to Africa Movement.

Usain Bolt — First man to run and break 100 and 200 metres records in an Olympic game.

Cindy Breakspeare — Former Miss World

Veronica Campbell — Olympic gold medalist at 200 metres at 2004 and 2008 Olympics.

Courtney Walsh — Former World record holder in test cricket – 519 wickets.

Guyana:

Sir Walter Rodney	Pan African Activist, famous for his thesis and book, 'How Europe Underdeveloped Africa'.
Clive Lloyd	Most successful cricket captain to play the game of cricket in modern times.

Cuba:

Fidel Castro	One of the most influential politicians of the second half of the 20th century.
Teofilo Stevenson	(Refer to greats of SVG) Three times Olympic Champion in heavy weight division in boxing.
Alberto Juantorena	Double gold medalist in the 400 and 800 metres in the 1976 Montreal Olympic games.
Ana Fidelia Quirot	Cuban 400 metres sprinter/gold medal in two consecutive Olympics. A demonstration of victory over defeat after having been involved in an almost fatal accident.

Belize:

Andy Palacio	Grammy award winner for indigenous music (Punta rock music).

Dominican Republic:

Felix Sanchez	400 meters hurdles

Haiti:

Toussaint L'Ouverture	The architect of the Haitian revolution – freed Haiti from slavery.

Bahamas:

Sydney Poitier

First African American to win an Oscar also credited for being involved in the first inter-racial kiss on the big screen.

Barbados:

Sir Garfield Sobers

Dubbed the greatest cricketer and all rounder ever to have played the game of Cricket

Journalist: What were your impressions of Cuba on arrival?

Dr. Toney: When I arrived in Havana City on the 17th September, 1987 at 9p.m my first impression was one of shock. There were so many Cubans walking the streets, eating ice-cream or just hanging out as we drove along the way to the intransit house for foreign students in playa. There were moments when Russian-made three wheel motorcycles sped past us and instantly the images of the German secret police flashed across my mind as I had first seen these vehicles in films of World War I and II. I had never seen these vehicles at home, so they remain quite vivid in my memory.

When I enquired about the number of persons on their verandas I was informed that they were members of the Committee for the Defense of the Revolution (CDR). These persons took turns in neighbourhood watch, and it was at this moment that the thought came to me that Cuba is the island that doesn't sleep.

Another aspect of Cuban life that fascinated me on arrival was the fact that Cubans throw away nothing. They are so industrious and innovative that they find use for anything and everything.

Journalist: I know Cuba is famous for its music and dance; did you have a chance to be a part of this aspect of the culture?

Dr. Toney: Yes, fortunately I learnt to appreciate and dance a little to the music. The music is very similar to calypso, the themes, octaves, scales and melodies are very similar. Percussion and brass section predominate in its music. Sometimes there is great synthesis of folk melodies in various musical arrangements. There are many great Cuban bands that have excelled internationally. These include groups like Los Van Van, Irakere and Bueña Vista Social Club (who won Grammy awards) and musicians like Silvio Rodriguez and Pablo Milanés never cease to keep the world from singing and dancing. Most Cuban musicians read music or have gone to music school. There are many full fledged musical symphonies with brass and modern instruments. The Cuban people are very rhythmical and will move to the slightest sound of a musical note and can party with very little culinary preparation. Música (music) is Cubans food and medicine

I was also thrilled to see the large collection of vintage cars still in working condition in Cuba. These are referred to by the Cubans as Macquina. Some of these cars include Chevy's, Ford, Buick and many more American brands stretching as far back as the 1930's. These are outdated anywhere and can only be seen in museums, while in Cuba they function efficiently still.

Looking at the traffic in Havana, you would think you are seeing a movie of the mafia in Miami during the pre-Castro times. And you know what is surprising, is that the Cuban mechanics like a friend of mine Pedro, are able to manufacture spare parts like brake shoes, disc pads, mufflers, radiators etc to keep these 'dinosaurs' on the road. Necessity is really the mother of invention in Cuba. Here you will understand quite clearly the difference between creativity and ingenuity. You will also appreciate the meaning of appropriate technology and science for living and production.

Sometimes to understand the linkages between Cuba and the United States, one has to go back to history. Most of my readers may not know this, but many American companies, especially fashion designers and clothing companies premiered their product in Havana even before the American market, and many Americans travelled to Cuba to shop during the era that the mafia controlled the hotels and tourist sector of the island's economy. Cuba was also one of the most travelled holiday destination for Americans. Many wealthy Americans travelled to Cuba for breakfast, lunch or dinner.

Journalist: Which Cuban landmark is the most interesting in your opinion?

Dr. Toney: El Morro stands out in my mind; this sixteenth century fortification built by Spain in Havana represents the most interesting landmark for the Cuban people. It symbolizes the continuous struggle of the Cuban people for self determination. It also embodies emancipation, independence, liberty and the pursuit of social justice. No one should go to Cuba and leave without visiting El Morro.

Journalist: What words of encouragement would you like to give to students who are contemplating a career in a foreign country or may be offered a scholarship to study in Cuba?

Dr. Toney: Well, if you were given a scholarship to study in a metropolitan or internationally accepted country where English is the first language, then I would say go for it. But if you wanted to learn another language and understand life and adversities, along with facing challenges and resilience in adversity, I would recommend Cuba. By studying in Cuba I can guarantee you will be a more humane professional and that you will be given a well rounded first-class education that will prepare you to face any challenge with a greater social conscience. Make no one deter you from a free education anywhere, for it is not easy paying back student loans, and at this moment I can write another book on that topic.

Journalist: What do you think makes the career of medicine so special?

Dr. Toney: A doctor is a special person in any society (along with nurses); we take care of you from conception to death. It is the most humane profession there is, of course I would have my bias (laughing). Doctors and nurses need to be cherished by any society and the same can be said about any profession, but I have to defend my profession first. Don't feel left out Neville, you are important too (laughing).

Journalist: Doc I know you have been practising medicine for some time now in St. Vincent and the Grenadines. How has the island benefited from your expertise?

Dr. Toney: Before I came back to the island, many of my patients had never heard about detoxification nor practised such a procedure on a regular basis. Today many of them manage the term and the procedure as though they are experts. By attending my clinic patients are familiar with the term and the process. We (Dr. Edmund Sealy and myself) were among the first to introduce Swedish bitters in St. Vincent. I know we would have contributed to the improvement of many lives. I think that in the area of fertility, I have been able to touch many lives. The poor and under-privileged, the rich and the poor have seen their dreams come to reality by having a child, some after many years of various attempts, others after repeated failure at invitro-fertilization. It's always a blessing to hold a child that you in some small way helped to become a reality. What's also very emotional is when these same children call you by your name and you realize in some way that their story was shared with them by their parents. They feel so close to you and at the same time they hold you in such high esteem and it's a wonderful feeling, and it's humbling to say the least.

Journalist: We are running out of time. Do you have any final words?

Dr. Toney: There's a French saying, gratitude is the memory of the heart. With this saying I would like to extend special thanks to all my patients who have trusted me with their lives in the past. I couldn't make it without you, thanks a trillion.

Journalist: I'm sorry Doc for creating this anti climax, but I think it's necessary before we end. Do you have any enemies Dr. Toney?

Dr. Toney: I personally do not waste time on the trivia of enmity, for even in the Bible it speaks of enemies. I would be naïve to think that I don't. I often read Psalms chapter 27 verse 2, "When the wicked, even my enemies and my foes came upon me to eat my flesh, they stumbled and fell."

Cuba's national poet José Martí once wrote, "It is sad to have no friend but it is worse to have no enemy, for if you have no enemy you have no light that shines on the world or qualities that are envied." I do not worry about my enemies, I'm more concerned about my friendemies, for those are more difficult to decipher and that's the reason when I pray I ask the Lord to show me my friends for I know he will guard me against my enemies.

Chapter 15

Obama the First Black President of the United States of America

In the summer of 2004, August to be exact, I was in Brooklyn in a restaurant where I met this middle aged man of Caucasian descent. We exchanged ideas, and spoke about America, its economy and its weaknesses and strengths as a nation. I then outlined my appreciation of the fiery speech delivered by the Junior Senator from Illinois, Barack Obama at the 2004 democratic convention held in July. We spoke at length about that speech of the Senator and I remembered vividly asking him, "Do you think the U.S.A will ever vote for a black President?" He looked at me a little perplexed and said sarcastically, "The last black President (Bill Clinton) did not do too badly but the American people are not prepared for another such President so soon." Then I interrupted him and asked, "What about a real African-American as you call us here in America?" He laughed with a surprised look," It shows you are not from here or even living here," So I introduced myself as being from St. Vincent and the Grenadines and he chuckled, " Oh you are from the islands, that's why." He went on, "When an African- American becomes the President of the U.S.A, I think this will herald the beginning of the second coming of the Lord and I know for sure that I'll be going back to Church."

I wonder if he has kept his promise or even if he has read or heard of Obama's book "The Audacity of Hope". Well the audacity of hope has finally turned to the audacity of Obama, for he has won the presidential elections of November 4th 2008, defeating his rival John McCain of the Republican party and was sworn in on the 17th January, 2009 as the 44th president of the USA. Simultaneously Barack became the first black president of the USA. Congratulations President Barack

Obama!

Most persons never imagined that in their wildest dream, nor in their lifetime they would have lived to see a black president, but I knew that day when it was announced that Barack Obama had won the presidency of the United States of America, that gentleman whom I had met in that restaurant would have remembered me vividly, there is no question about that, for I believe that I was the first person who had caused him to imagine that one day there was a possibility of this becoming reality. Even when I heard the news I "pinched" myself and asked "Am I dreaming?" America has reemerged as a thriving mature democracy which is slowly moving beyond race and in so doing has fulfilled the dreams of Martin Luther King and kept steadfast to the saying, "America is a Land of opportunity". It has led the developed world by example to show that all men were created equal. If my mom was alive to see how Obama had won the presidency, I know she would say to me, "You see Andy, class is forever once you are alive".

Obama the quintessential male of the 21ˢᵗ century

Jane, Joan and Janet were selling under the mango tree, just in front of my gate. They were conversing while I was passing, so I took the liberty to join in the discussion.

Jane explained in a soft voice, "With all due respect to Michelle, Malia and Sasha, Barrack is my kind of man." I couldn't help interjecting.

"What do you mean by that?" I asked.

So she continued, "Look he is relatively young, handsome, athletically built, full six foot, plus well groomed and always well attired. His baritone voice coupled with his eloquence and confidence in delivery mixed with a persuasive tone and vocal rhythm make me vulnerable as a woman. He is my ideal man. I need a man like Barrack Obama."

Joan exclaimed, "You are so pathetic, you seem not to get it right. Your ideal man is so superficial; no wonder you are always having problems in your relationships. You seem not to go below the surface. To me Barack is more interesting than how you have painted him. A woman of substance looks deeper to find her real man. What impresses me about President Obama is his un- stuttering ability to communicate his dreams and aspirations; he's bold, I mean unabashed, unflappable with an extremely self assuming nature. He is so endearing. I must add that in spite of all his achievements, he hasn't lost the common touch. This is the irony that I look for in my man. "You two girls are wrong."

Janet interrupted, "You are no better than Jane. Both of you need to look at the finer qualities in a man. President Obama to me embodies qualities like my father. He cares about his family which makes him so humane. Yes he's humble, eloquent and has a captivating 'pen'. Barrack is a great time manager and that's what impresses me most. He finds time for work and time to play. I believe strongly that Obama is quite a virile man, and to me that's one of the greatest qualities that a man can have. To Michelle, have no fear, I'm just reflecting on the wonderful creation of the Lord. He is to me the quintessential male of the 21st century."

Chapter 16

Different Moods of Dr. Chester Toney

Life is

----- Martinique 1994

Life is short, life is long

Life is love, life is none

Life s the sum of glorious uncertainties

Life is bitter, life is sweetLife is sorrow, life is fun

Life is loving a beautiful lady

And ensuring that she knows it

Life is saying goodbye to a loved one

Life is caring for someone you love

Life is singing upon hearing your favourite song

Life is hoping for a brighter tomorrow

Life is something we can never define

Because life signifies different things for different people

Life is what you make it

Some say life is like a fire, it starts burning then goes out

I say life is about knowing and loving the Creator

As you love yourself and your neighbour

Life is understanding that one day you will die

And in the midst of life you are in death

Life is like a see-saw,

One moment you're up the next moment you're down

Life is what happens the moment you are born and the day you die

And on this stage we all must play our part

Life is having a voracious appetite for living

Life is faith and leaning not on your own understanding

Life is like a puzzle, you have to find the pieces to complete the picture

For no one can do it for you, they can only assist you

Life is success and failure turned upside down

Life is a struggle for everyone

Life was made for living, enjoy it ……………………..

You

----- Kingston, Jamaica 1992

I have dreams of loving you,

Illusions of holding you

Strange feelings of seeing you

Doubts about meeting you

Great urgency to converse with you

Shivering feelings of hearing you

I'm overjoyed to share with you

I have steaming passion to be with you

Uncontrollable desires of wanting to smell you

Great necessity to learn about you

Crazy things to do to you

I would like to massage and caress you

Making breakfast in bed just for you

A bubble bath and candlelight dinner, me and you

I'm yearning to be part of you

And I want to feel the woman within you

In person, time and space I must have you

God knows how much I need you

God bless the day I set my eyes on you

I need you to experience how it feels, me being in love with you

On the contrary that you become me and I become you.

Until the end I will always love you

And today as always I am thinking about you

Sometimes I look in the mirror and all I see is you

Sometimes I shower believing the soap is you

Then after my shower my towel becomes you

It is so immense the reality I have of you

That presently I relive the history of my future with you

And I see the fertilization of me and you

In a nutshell, another me to replenish the earth and another you.

Hairouna, Land of the Blessed

----- Milton Keynes, Buckinghamshire UK, 2002

I am a man from the land where birds and butterflies still soar freely

In an atmosphere pregnant with tranquility

Where untamed jackfish and tri-tri still roam, waiting

To be captured from the sea and river mouth destined for the pot

The land where bananas, fruits and vegetables are grown organically

The land where God's cricket, bullfrog and parrots Amazona guildingii

still make a joyful noise in symphony

The land where spirits of Chatoyer and Duvalle still battle heroically

and incessantly against foreign domination

The land where beauty is unspoilt, untouched, and uncontrollable

Friendly people abide in natural lingering luxury

Lavished by natural decadence of delicious foods

Saturated by fresh air

A land where there is no such thing as time

And trees and flowers are not afraid

To show themselves before the golden sun

With all their ostentatious colours

Hairouna where coconut trees guard hills and valleys

And breadfruit trees are five star generals

The La Soufriere stands majestically over the land and sea

As a reminder of God's ever presence

Have you ever dreamt of a land where the beaches yearn

to caress your body, and the sun your skin?

Search no more, welcome to Hairouna

The island where the pirates came to plunder

But had to leave all their treasures behind

Friendly people, rich soil, turquoise waters,

pure clean air, tasty dishes, did I mention grass?

The land where the best grass grows

I mean medicinal plants in her old botanical gardens

Home of the blessed Hairouna, land of my birth

Sovereign ground of Yurumein!

I surrender my passport and all travel documents

With no fuss if you do not return them

For you give me love, joy, peace, and happiness

Many left your shores for bigger cities

I am Vincy, here is where I call home

Some tear you to pieces, they say you are no fun

Truly here is where I belong

Some say your money gone funny

But I say here is where my heart is

Hairouna, we are together through thick and thin

Even though I may stray you will always be my home

For I am true son of your soil

We are in this thing together

So without further ado

Hairouna, I do

I do love you

God bless Hairouna Land of the blessed

Barry, my brother from another mother

-----Kingstown, St. Vincent, February 2009

Barry, my blood brother you live in me

Barry my brother I live in you

You are the symbolic shadow of

Martin, Booker T, Brother Bob,

Garvey, Carver, Nelson, J.F.K., Rosa,

Stokeley, Chatoyer, and not forgetting Dad.

Barry, some say you are a Muslim, others

Say you are a Christian. I even overheard

Someone saying you are a Buddhist. Who do you say you are Barry?

Do you tell them you have unseen relatives?

You see Barry, you can choose your friends but not your family.

Did you tell them Barry that you have relatives scattered all over Africa,

Europe, North and South America

And not forgetting the land of the blessed SVG

I've heard so much about you even though I've not really met you.

After Dad died I yearned intensely to know you and

finally in 2004 I saw you on television at the convention,

you were eloquent, fiery, and persuasive with your baritone voice.

You reminded me of daddy, I believe he lives in you

You don't play cricket like me and my brothers.

I see you play basketball and you're great, you know your game.

I hear you like pies just like me,

my favourite though is yam pie, just like Usain, what's yours?

Barry, you dance well you've got the moves

Whenever we meet I will teach you how to dance calypso and soca.

You are now a fine man. I see you didn't walk in daddy's footsteps.

You are with your family and that's what counts.

You are the vessel for those who want to change this unjust world.

'Yes we can', change you can believe in

We know the battle has just begun.

You are the mouthpiece for correcting injustice at home and abroad.

Don't forget your father's Land Africa, and the black man

The microphone for those who experience poverty

Amidst enormous vile material prosperity

One lady said you are the last human beacon of light to "life, liberty and

the pursuit of happiness," in a world ravished by racial inequity, religious

warfare, political instability and the global economic meltdown.

Barry, one of my neighbours said that you are so cool in adversity

You must be smoking "medically approved filter-tipped marijuana."

I know better my brother; your 'friendemies' swear you are on Xanac.

Don't bother my brother, they will never understand

that you are blessed to handle success, conflict and contradictions.

Some say you are socializing capitalism, so what's wrong with that?

My brother Barry, you are in me so too is Michelle, Sasha, Malia

You are my brother from another mother

Your voice is my voice; your blood is my blood.

Thank you for uplifting the family name, Mom and Dad are smiling

You inspire all our children including Chester Jr. and Je-vonni,

that's the true measure of success for a leader.

I remain the brother you have never met, candid, emotional, and real.

Sorry I just can't contain these joyous tears...............................

The magnitude of your victory is too immense to measure and you

Have laid the foundation for a window to the future.

After all, you are spreading the wealth around.

The vampires who live by 'sucking' blood of sufferers are angry

They were the ones who chattered, "Greed is good!"

Don't bother about the poor

They will be taken care of by natural selection

They are now shouting, "Need is bad!"

But you know what, the sufferers have no more blood,

So the vipers need you to bail them out

That's exploitation in reverse, but that's the nature of the beast

May God bless you abundantly.

The seven steps to success

-----Queens, New York, USA August 2007

Power is knowledge not abuse of knowledge

Knowledge is strength not the prostitution of strength

Strength is faith not the indifference to faith

Faith is hope not glimmers of hope

Hope is virtue not the quest for virtue

Virtue is humility not professed humility

Humility is love not the love of possessions nor positions

Love is success not just material success and

Success is eternal

Cuba

-----Vedado Cuba 1998

You were called the Paris of the West

The birthplace of socialism in the west

Land of Marti, Marceo, Gómez, and lately Fidel

Land of palm trees, home of the best cigars

Land of resistance, the sugar cane capital of the world

Resting place for Hemmingway and Picasso

Situated in the entrance of the Gulf of Mexico

In plain Caribbean Sea

With Haiti in the east, Yucatan in the West

Florida's peninsula in the north and Jamaica to the south

Friend of so many impoverished nations

Your mountains rise strategically and symbolically out of your belly

Sierra Maestra, Escambrey, El Pico Real del Turquino

To name a few; you are truly the Hope of the Antilles

For your people possess the heart of diamond,

Platinum, Gold, Nickel, for sure and Uranium

They are your greatest gifts from God

You were the catalyst for dismantling Apartheid

At the same time you are the origin of Song

"Oh Beny Moret how I miss you"

The heart beat of Guaguancó, Mambo, Cha-cha-cha, and Danzón

In synthesis the university of struggle

You are the good, the bad, the ugly and the sexy

From Guantanamo to Pinar del Río including

La Isla de la Juventud not forgetting La Habana my second home

Sons and daughters of Che Guevara

You are Cuba and can be no other

Because, "to die for the homeland is to live."

¡Patria O Muerte!

¡Venceremos!

Can you imagine a world without Cuba?

No I can't

May God be with you

A vincy's opinion on being black in America and beyond

----- Arnos Vale, St. Vincent, 2009

You are not a "nigger" as you are forced to believe

A nigger's history, can only be traced back to slavery

You are more than the descendants of the remnants

Of those who survived the middle passage

Yes, most of us came from the same ship

Taking the same trip

And felt the same whip

Grandchildren of the doors of "no return"

You are above racial "profiling"

Take the shackles off of your mind

My sisters, you are no "nappy-headed" woes

My brothers, you are no "banana eating" jungle monkey

Your colour does not make you less than nor more than anyone else

It just makes you different

Take your place in a world that is afraid of you

Not for what you are, but for what you can become

A world afraid to mentor you in wealth creation and innovation

Yes, they are afraid to teach you "not to sell yourself cheaply"

Not to fear failure and to stand on your own two feet

Love yourself! Hunger for knowledge and success!

The man who wins is the man who sees the end and not the journey

Strive for love, courage, respect and faith

Endeavour to be happy, have compassion

Once you can dream it, believe me you can do it

Don't forget your history while keeping steadfast to your destiny

My sister, understand and cherish motherhood

My brother, fatherhood is serious business

And in your hands lie the architects of the next generation

Plan for tomorrow by spending less than you earn

Save what you don't spend and invest a part of what you saved

Blacks in America and beyond!

How could you not cry for Darfur and Ethiopia?

How could you not weep for Haiti?

How could you not weep for the people of Zimbabwe?

How could you not beg for the unjust embargo to be lifted off Cuba?

How can you have talks at WTO and forget the Caribbean?

How could you slumber and don't think about the impoverished people
from all parts of the world?

Black people, White people, Yellow people and the in-betweens

A shackled man anywhere is a threat to freedom everywhere

My blood brothers, stop being a blind visionary

Not because the vehicle has changed velocity means you are better

For you're not, you are still in the back seat

And even though it appears that you're in the driver's seat in the USA

It doesn't mean you are in control

You're a man, black like the ace of spades and has many shades

Your wooly hair is black and comely

Your full size nose and lips define you

THE JOURNEY OF A THOUSAND MILES BEGINS WITH A
SINGLE STEP
BLACK IS BEAUTIFUL TOO, WE ARE ONE PEOPLE, ONE
RACE, ONE DESTINY

Politrickans

----- *Arnos Vale, St. Vincent, August 12th 2009*

Ah gwine vote, ah gwine mark me X

Nah ask me who me gwine vote fa

Dat ah between me an God

Remember yuh neva gee me blocks,

Nar lumber nar galvanize

fo put on e little addition pan me one room board house

for me wife an me ten pickney an dem

Whey you say, me mus throw water pan dat

well ah guess yuh ready to help me now.

Ok Sir, well the ole people dem does say, ah bird in de han

Worth a million in the bushes

So whey yuh fo gee me, gee me now

E las time me see yuh bin five years ago

Yuh nah kno if me eat, if me bin sick

Yuh na even kay if my Monday bin fall pan Sunday

Me bin glimpse yuh when yuh bin jus tek office

Yuh bin ah drive thru the village under speed in ah yuh big jeep

With e dark glass an dem roll up

Me see yuh no longer have the jalopy.

Hear me now, "Wait, nah me representor gone day?"

Benwood an dem boys say yuh jus keek yuh horn

Yuh na even stop fuh gee them ah drink ah Preddie

All dem time day me house roof ah leak, an hear me

"Boy, me wish me representor ah pass cross fuh gee me ah pull out."

Ar yo really tek poor people fuh fool

Dem say ah promise is a comfort to a fool

An if ah so, me nah gwine be no fool no more

Well ah gwine mark me X nah watch me so perplexed

Me bin vote fuh yuh, fuh alleviate my poverty

But e look like my vote alleviate yours

Too long poor people ah spin tap in ah mud

Too long e pot ah cook and e food nah nuff

Nah because the Lord say

The poor will always be in our midst

Ah yuh nah ha none time wid arwe

Well from now on me ah vote fuh the party in power

Wat is dat? Yes, PIP, Party In Power

Me nah spit fire fuh non ah yo again

Me gwine mark me X an demand

Whosoever in power pay me my dues

My vote will be constant me nah joke,

No favour, no vote

But wait, after all my vote cannot be bought nar sold

My vote is more precious dan silver, diamond and gold

My vote does mek big man bawl like little boy

My vote does mek king vacate them throne

My vote does mek thieving politrickans tek dem belly make boat

My vote does turn poor man into rich man over night.

Politrickans, when ah yo get in power

Ay yuh does drink the Forgetful Champagne

An the whiskey call Amnesia

Ay yuh does forget whey ay yuh come from, who bin ay yuh friends

Some ah you does forget ay yuh name

Cause ay yuh nar war answer to ay yuh name

Unless e hah honourable infront of um

Moreso, the cariabbean politrickans

The more all yuh look to England

The more Westminister haunting we

You cause people to go blind by colours

Den tun around an want dem to be colour blind

Me gwine mark me X and this is me an God business

Anyhow, whey yuh say yuh have something fuh me

Me want a scholarship fuh me first gal pickney

Who jus done school an me second boy war go in ah de army

Me hah two bwoy whey nar wuk no way

Try get one wuk fuh demm gimme

Both ah dem hah ten O'levels

So yuh see if yuh really war help me

Yuh go gimme at least some cement, blocks, galvanize and lumber

Then we will do the honourable thing

And cast we vote for yuh

And so yuh will get five arwe vote

When arwe mark we X, we nah business who vex

And e wire ben' and e story end

Sir Mango from Stubbs

----- Belmont, St. Vincent, August 13ᵗʰ 2009

Mango sweet, mango sour, mango has an electric power.

These are memorable words that we rehearsed in our childhood

To convey our love and appreciation for mangoes

It often marvels me how a small nation like SVG

Can have such a wide variety of mangoes

I reminisce on my childhood experiences

And the names of these mangoes still reverberate in my mind

Debique, Starchy, Imperial, Celon, Wyllie

Sour Mango, Little Salt, Scotch, Cattle Tongue, Georgie

Bastard, Sweet Gems, Custard Mango, Julie

Grafted, Cat Seed, Tenor Mark, Horsey

Peach, Cattle Mango, Paul Over, Red Breast, Goutie

Turpentime, Trinidad, Shilling, Wym, Young Girl Bubby

Magum, Scratch, Buccorn, Collins, Tom Puss, Hairy

Bubby Nipple, Red Breast, Rotton Head, Nelly

Water Wash, Leather Skin, Wall, Palowie

Scottle, Round Mango, Whitey, Big Bitch, Yamey

And the list goes on unendingly.

Mango must be an unsung hero in vincy

For it has stopped many poor people children from going hungry

Some eat mango for dinner, lunch and tea

And end up with an upset belly

You can make mango juice, jam, nectar and even jelly

But if it were not for mango,

A lot of poor people would have died already in SVG

So, sing hail to Sir Mango, his Excellency

For preserving life in our country

Scrambled Eggs

----- Port of Spain, Trinidad, 2007

Come and break your fast

At the White House with Style and Grace

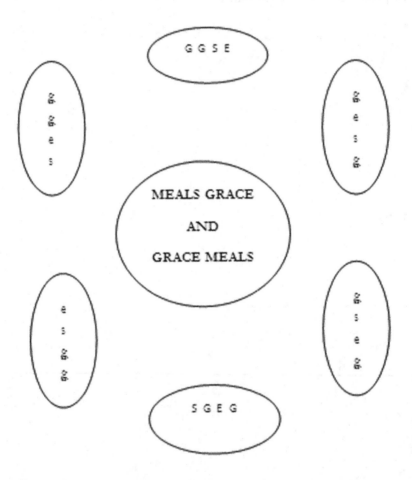

Black, red, white and blue

You

----- *Kingston, Jamaica 1992*

I have dreams of loving you,

Illusions of holding you

Strange feelings of seeing you

Doubts about meeting you

Great urgency to converse with you

Shivering feelings of hearing you

I'm overjoyed to share with you

I have steaming passion to be with you

Uncontrollable desires of wanting to smell you

Great necessity to learn about you

Crazy things to do to you

I would like to massage and caress you

Making breakfast in bed just for you

A bubble bath and candlelight dinner, me and you

I'm yearning to be part of you

And I want to feel the woman within you

In person, time and space I must have you

God knows how much I need you

God bless the day I set my eyes on you

I need you to experience how it feels, me being in love with you

On the contrary that you become me and I become you.

Until the end I will always love you

And today as always I am thinking about you

Sometimes I look in the mirror and all I see is you

Sometimes I shower believing the soap is you

Then after my shower my towel becomes you

It is so immense the reality I have of you

That presently I relive the history of my future with you

And I see the fertilization of me and you

In a nutshell, another me to replenish the earth and another you.

Me

-----Bridgetown, Barbados, 2007

When you look at me

You never see the real me

You see a figment of your imagination of me

You see an image that you think is me

An image that says so little or nothing about me

Except an erroneous perception of me

Even when my pain and anguish try to engulf me

I know you do not see the love and humanity in me

My lack of jewelry and bodily apparels speaks volumes about me

For when I entered this world, all I had was me

No titles, no accolades nor degrees were bestowed upon me

It was just me and only me.

I've lived so humble that no one noticed me

My loved ones were the greatest treasures to me

As my life ebbs away only the gifts of precious memories sustain me

I bleed not my heart for vanity as this means so little to me

For at the end of the journey all I'll take home is me.

Missing You

----- Richmond Hill, Kingstown, 2006

Dedicated to Jennifer

You have gone for several days now

And the windows of my room seem wider than before

The walls appear to hold me captive in my own space

As I caress the virtual silhouette of your warm embrace

The deafening silence of your absence engulf my being

Like a fish out of water, frantically clinging to life

Since you've been gone my nights are longer

My days are dreary and unendingly misty blue

Without a shadow of a doubt I'm missing you ....

The pain is real, my heart is broken in a million pieces

That only you can put together again

From the moment you were gone

You took half of me with you

I know you will return

But the waiting feeling is not fine

Every second is like a thousand years without you

And I console myself believing you're still here with me

Just like a sun flare our distance is only temporary

I miss your smile, your dishes and honey laced kisses

I even miss your heated argument surprisingly!

Your king has lost his kingly character

And the throne on which he sits is of no significance to his reign

Behold my loneliness!

Who is a king if he doesn't have a queen?

The inaudible murmur of your absence thrills me

A chain of lonely nights and miserable moments border my existence

Am afraid to sleep for fear of you evading my consciousness

A thousand years from now if you're not here

I'll be still missing you

No one knows the complete void I feel within

Even though I pretend am smiling

Am choking on every conceivable thought of your absence

If loving you seems crazy, I don't want to be intelligent nor sane

I peer at your fictitious replica on the wall

Hoping by divine intervention you'll be mine once more

Even though am in company, am alone

P.s. My Cousin Who "Fathered" Me
----- Kingstown, 2009

From Byrea he emerged with a passion to be somebody,

With unwavering discipline, determination and strong personality

He climbed to the pinnacle of the education ministry

And played a pivotal role in moulding the society, spiritually

Touching many lives as a human being with dignity

A Vincentain who gave of himself, and did so selflessly

Pure in heart with no love for vanity

Grounded deeply in the principles of humility

An intransigent commandant against ignorance and illiteracy

A man of extreme moral integrity

Who demonstrated a rare Vincentain diplomacy

And took time off to help all and sundry

Aman who was a father to many though none biologically

And exhibited true love to them continuously

Digging deep into his own pockets and giving generously

Rest in peace Uncle Festus sincerely

The whole world mourns on the death of an upright Toney

We will miss the dean of the Toney family

But most of all I will remember you as the cousin who fathered me.

New York, New York

----- Kingstown, 2009

They say you are the capital of the world

Because you are known to every boy and girl

New York New York, so uncontainable they named you twice

A city where the world pay your price

Some to visit, others for your sugar and spice.

The city of opportunities where men behave like mice

In a split second a beggar becomes wealthy

By virtue of the stock exchange everything vanishes instantly

New York the city that doesn't sleep

For that's the price you pay and the discount you keep

New York, the melting pot of many cultures

Where losers become winners and winners are potential losers

New York, where stampedes occur on the rush hour

The rat race of trains, vehicles and people make a country boy cower.

New York, where some disputes are settled with a nine millimeter

And not with the contents of a man's character

Stilettos shod ladies dressed in Armani, Dolce and Gabana and Gucci

Can only be dined and wined with fame and big money

And in the wee hours if you're lucky

Every thing is for free

You're not a perfect city, but you're a special place to be

For you are the leader of western democracy

Brooklyn, Broadway and the Statue of Liberty

You are the heartbeat of the big apple, New York City

I love New York, but does New York love me?

Magic in Mathematics

----- *Kingstown, August 2009*

Think of a number

Multiply it by 2

Add 4, then multiply by 3

Are you finish?

Now, to that result

Divide by 6

Yes 6

No. You don't need a calculator

Come, just have a little patience

Have you finish the division?

Now, subtract the number you chose

Isn't your answer 2?

This is close to magic isn't it?

Well this is mathematics!

What you said, mathemagic?

No this is simple arithmetic

Something so simple yet so mystic

But that's the power of mathematics

My farewell letter to Cuba and the Cuban People (Translated from Spanish) ----- Vedado, Havana, 16th September 1998, 9:00 p.m.

Dear Cuba,

I reminisce now on my arrival to your landscape and capital city in 1987. The uncertainty of my sojourn from Hairoun to Havana, the rebellious nature of this journey, the joy of pursuing the dream of becoming a doctor, learning a foreign language all featured in my mind intertwined with a relentless quest for academic success.

I recall many of the great moments spent with you and how I was able to discover many of your hidden treasures within you that the world is yet to enjoy. Treasures which include your food, dances, music, paintings, poets and other cultural art forms; your history, your struggle as a nation, your education, sports and healthcare and most of all your people; their warmth, love and ingenuity. It was Pablo Milanes who said, "I do not live in a perfect society." And I do agree with him whole heartedly. Carlos Varela on the other hand highlighted, "I do not have superman, I have Elpidio Valdés." Expressing what makes him uniquely Cuban. Presently my heart is rending as I remember so many friends I have made and will lose partially.

It hurts me to say goodbye after ten years. Tomorrow will be exactly eleven years since I left St. Vincent and the Grenadines in pursuit of a dream. The dream is now reality but the journey towards this reality was filed with joy and pain. Though today the journey feels joyous, the uncertainty of the future lingers in my thoughts. So now this journey has ended the future seems even more frightening now than it was then. Finding a job in my homeland as the first Cuban trained specialist is a struggle that I look forward to face head on.

I have kept my end of the bargain with you and also that with my family and friends and it hurts to bid you farewell. God knows the pain I feel inside and nobody knows it but me. Cuba I've given you some of the better years of my life and I'm grateful to be afforded the opportunity. In return you have given me so many loving memories laced with nostalgia too numerous to mention. You have played your part well in nurturing me during most of my adult life and I'm cognizant that you have given me sufficient training in living and production, and overcoming adversity. Most of all you have taught me how to struggle and how to sustain life in general.

Many of my friends from other lands were unfortunate in completing the journey, sometimes surrendering when the going got rough. Even though they are not here to celebrate with us tonight, we still remember them and cherish the friendships and fraternal bonds. I have lived fantastic days with you even in those times of "special periods", the effects of El niño and various hurricanes that never ceased to ravish your land. All good things come to an end and logically the end has arrived for us to part.

I have left behind many of my godsons and goddaughters and many other children with my name as a reminder of my presence on your soil, and the hundreds of boys and girls who were delivered by these hands are all indelible prints that have marked the passage of my medical sojourn. I know you will never hesitate to accept me as a son, a brother and a comrade for I've fought many battles by your side and I have my scars to show.

It was just one week ago that I learnt that I have a son with one of your daughters. This means legally I am bonded to you. It is this duty that exists now that makes it even more painful to separate from you. I have little material acquisitions with me for they mean so little to me at this time. Instead I have gained other possessions which are more valuable to humanity. These include the unapologetic quest for success of the soul and spirit.

Hairoun is the land I love, Cuba is the land I grew to love and I pledge to you that in my quest for success I will always remember you. Though we do not always share the same political persuasion this should never prevent us from being friends to the end. It hurts me to go but I know it will hurt me more to let you go, so without further unnecessary waste of ink and paper as words will never express my true love and gratitude towards you.

Until victory always

Patria O muerte!

Your Vincentian son and comrade

Chester

Significant Notes about – Dr. Chester Toney

1. The Toney family was the first family from Marriaqua to have sent all their children to Petersville Primary School (a private school) in Kingstown. From the late 60's to 1983 the family had a child or more attending the school.

2. I was the only student of the St. Vincent Grammar School in 1981 who was disqualified from participating in the high jump. According to the then headmaster Stanley Campbell, because I was jumping "too dangerously", he (headmaster) instructed the games master to discontinue any jump by me (Chester Toney). However, the following year, I was rewarded by placing third in the high jump in my division.

3. I was a member of the photography club headed by Lennox Adams and including members like Elliot Williams, Jasmine Malcolm, Andrew Rogers and Ian Rogers.

4. I represented St. Vincent and the Grenadines in the 1985 mock UN assembly in Jamaica and was the first Vincentian to be trained as a UNESCO club organizer.

5. At University I was an avid half marathon runner having defeated some of the university favourites like Kenya, Mozambique and Ethiopia and placed second to Zambia.

6. I was the only Caribbean student on campus who participated in Judo while in the pre-clinical years of my career.

7. I was a dramatist and participated in an off campus drama group. I played Julius Caesar in the Shakespearan tale, and most recently Delroy in "Oh Daddy", a play written and directed by Marc Ederich and Ruth Boerger in 2008.

8. In 1994 I achieved the best results in Obstetrics and Gynaecology for any foreign student. This later facilitated my direct entry into the specialty.

9. I was the first Vincentian doctor to specialize in Cuba 1994-1998.

10. Between 1990 and 1991 I was the only Vincentian student in Cuba and was head of the student council for six months.

11. I was nicknamed Millo (pronounced Me-yo) in my residency years due to the fact that I gave away all my material possessions every time I ventured out of Cuba. Millo is the short form for millonario (millionaire) in Spanish.

12. I demonstrated great business acumen when I conducted business between Jamaica and Cuba selling Jamaica and Bob Marley T-shirts from 1995-1997. My niche market was among the African students studying there. Proceeds from the sale of these t-shirts assisted in financing my medical career.

13. I was known in the St. Vincent Grammar School for being a fierce competitor in arm wrestling. Other fierce competitors were Peter Providence, Dowie Cato, Rohan Toney, Vincent Reid and Sylvanus Morgan-Horne.

14. I played football for various forms while at Grammar School. I am mostly remembered for Mark 'Bamboo' Child in a football match 4-science against 5-science. Even though we lost the match (4-science) the highlight of the game was the collision between Mark Child and myself which resulted in Child, who was recognized as one of the most formidable defenders in school, falling flat in a pool of mud on that rainy Saturday at the Richmond Hill playing field.

15. Of all the persons who went to Grammar school, I still maintain close relationship with Stanley Browne, Cameron Stephens, Sylvanus Morgan-Horne, Gary Young, Peter Providence, Elvin Jackson, Michael Seales and Curtis Bascombe. I also have an enduring friendship with Julian Farrel who attended the St. Martin's Secondary School.

16. I trained hundreds of medical students in my residency years at the Gonzales Corro OB/GYN hospital from 1994-1998.

17. I produced many scientific papers while in Cuba. Some of these were about sleep and health, fibroids and pregnancy, ultrasound in the Gynaecological patient P-P-G (Cuban version of Ateromixol) and its use in sexual dysfunction, Alternative Medicine versus Conventional Medicine.

18. In 1990 I met Stokeley Carmichael (Kwame Toure) and Akinyele Umoja in Havana while attending an international symposium on 'Malcolm X speaks in the nineties'. Also present were members of the black community in the USA who had vowed to begin the pursuit of a black president in the United States of America.

19. In Jamaica I was fortunate to have met Carl Bradshaw who was coincidentally my neighbour while living in Portmore. Mr. Bradshaw has acted in many famous Jamaican movies including 'Third World Cop'.

20. Also while in Jamaica I met the reggae singer Kiddus I who gave me many tips on singing reggae music. Kiddus I acted in the movie "Rockers".

Photo Gallery

The historic photos of Earl 'Ole George' Daniel and Joel Butcher, supervised medically by Dr. Chester Toney on 14th March 2005 can be viewed in the following pages. These photos of persons from all walks of life of the Vincentian society can be seen including the Prime Minister Hon. Ralph E. Gonsalves, the opposition leader Hon. Arhim Eustace, government Ministers, businessmen, the press and humble folks on National Heroes Day in St. Vincent and the Grenadines. No one before had walked continuously without sleeping for six days. This record we broke subsequently in Jamaica walking for seven days was repeated again in St. Vincent in 2007 without any acceptance by the Guinness Book of Records. We proceeded for eight days in Central Park, New York. After breaking the world record on four consecutive occasions Earl 'Ole George' Daniel and Joel Butcher were unable to awake the record keepers of the Guinness Book of World Record.

Like our heroes before, our team came up against injustices and blatant disrespect for our efforts and unwavering persistence. It is my belief that our efforts should be recorded in history so that our great grand children do not feel that their fore parents did nothing to place St. Vincent and the Grenadines on the world stage.

Come on Guinness! Shame on you! Stop denying a people its rightful place in world history!

History in the making, the flag of SVG carried
with pride. It is not the size of the country but
the quality of its citizens (athletes) that matters

Final day of the record breaking walk at Arnos Vale.
Please note the arrow showing Ole George

Police motorcycles from the Royal St. Vincent and the Grenadines
Police Force precede the walk along Murrays Road.

Ole George on the left and Joel Butcher
on the right after finishing their walk

Conclusion

Symbiosis

All of my disappointments, even the most miniscule and most absurd were very important in moulding my life today. It was important that I express the realities of my sojourn from Marriaqua to Havana and back. I am no self made person, the words of the African saying best describe my unapologetic quest for success. "Until the Lion tells his own tales, the tales of the hunt will always glorify the hunter".

This book is written so that you the reader who don't really know me will get a glimpse of who I am, my life, triumphs and obstacles, dreams and aspirations. No one has a better story to tell about you than you yourself. To those who think I am arrogant, full of myself, I forgive you. You simply do not know the real me. For if you knew me, you would never think that way about me. Just as Jaques Rogge thought that the star athletic performer at the 2008 Beijing Olympics, Jamaican Usain Bolt was arrogant and full of himself even after three world record breaking performances. Bolt celebrated in true Caribbean style and remains unapologetic up to this day.

I too remain unapologetic after being associated with four world record breaking performances which Joel Butcher and Earl 'Ole George' Daniel achieved in endurance walking (walking without sleep) also done in true Caribbean style.

It's amazing how "the more things change the more they remain the same." (Remember Hitler's response to Jessie Owens' performance in the 1936 Olympics in Berlin Germany). The record breaking performances of Ole George and Butcher and also Usain Bolt, reinforce my belief that Caribbean people can achieve anything at the highest level on the world stage. "The 22-year old Bolt became the first man ever to break world records in both the 100 and 200 meters at the games. In the 100, Bolt celebrated the last 20 meters, but still set a record at 9.69 seconds. However, he put his all in the 200 m. race and won by the largest margin in Olympic history!! His time 19.30 seconds and broke the legendary Michael Johnson's world record." (Jet Magazine, September 8th, 2008)

We may be small geographically; however it is not the size of the country that counts but the magnitude of the passion that burns within its people to do great works. In conclusion, for those whom I may have hurt unknowingly, I am sorry, but this still does not change my objectives, as I still remain humble and unapologetically humane.

My unapologetic quest for success if filed with the knowledge that wherever and whenever I trod the road to success, I have to remember Ephesians 6:12, "For we wrestle not against flesh and blood, but against principalities, against powers, against the rulers of the darkness of this world, against spiritual wickedness in high places." From logical deduction, when a turtle sits on the back of a chair, we know he did not get there all by himself, so too is the attainment of success especially when it is sought after diligently and with an attitude.

In the quest along this tiresome and lonely road you will create enemies but you must be shod with blood, sweat and tears encountered along this strenuous journey of excruciating pain while bearing in mind that the same people you meet on your way up are the very same ones you will meet on your way down for on earth nothing lasts forever. Every single footstep along the way should continue with faith and single-minded determination. The key to success is knowledge and the proper utilization of this new found weapon to do good and not evil in every waking moment of our daily existence. The haters of success are never on vacation, they don't take a day off nor do they ask for a recess. The quest should always be embraced by the overwhelming attitude that success is a must and failure is not an option. Just as the hymn writer says, "I shall not be, I shall not be moved", so too should be your attitude for in this hostile world even with an attitude you should remain paradoxically unpretentious.

For all who aspire to be successful one day just as I do, the words of Charles Kettering should be your guiding principle "You cannot stub your toe standing still, the faster you go the more chances you have of stubbing your toe, but the more chances you have of getting somewhere." This hostile world is not accommodating to the humble at heart, mind and spirit who charters a course toward success.

Until the victory, the struggle continues relentlessly keeping focus on the words of Bob Marley'

> *Get up, Stand up*
>
> *Stand up for your rights*
>
> *Get Up, Stand up*
>
> *Never give up the fight*

GOD BLESS!

3rd December, 2009 – 12:59 a.m.

Chester Toney

Carriere, Marriaqua

St. Vincent W.I.

P.O. Box 2366

drcltoney@hotmail.com

www.chestertoney.com

784-485-6045 (office)

784-455-3513 (cellular)

784-485-6945 (fax)

PHOTO GALLERY – ST. VINCENT AND THE GRENADINES

Come to St. Vincent and the Grenadines where we spell tourist as M-Y-F-R-I-E-N-D

The Botanical Gardens – The oldest botanical
garden in the Western Hemisphere

Amazona guildingii – The national bird of
St. Vincent and the Grenadines

Black Point Tunnel, built by slave labour and was
dug through volcanic rocks. This tunnel is over
300ft long and was constructed in 1815.

A view of the Marriaqua Valley – once considered to be the bread
basket of St. Vincent. Coincidentally, here is where is was born.

St. Mary's Roman Catholic Cathedral, Kingstown

Anglican Cathedral, Kingstown

Methodist Church, Kingstown

The nineteenth century fortification built in 1803. This was used as part of the setting of one of the battle scenes in the movie Pirates of the Caribbean

Black sand beach on the windward coast of St. Vincent.
Some of the finest surfing waters in the Caribbean

Owia Salt Pond

One of our many beautiful waterfalls on the island of St. Vincent

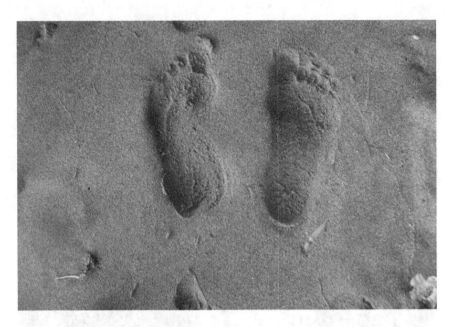

My footprints on the land that I love and cherish

Arnos Vale Sporting Complex - Arguably the most picturesque cricket grounds in the world. In the background lie the Grenadine islands, part setting for Pirates of the Caribbean sequel 1, 2 and 3

Some of the beaches of St. Vincent and the Grenadines which were
used as part of the filming of the Pirates of the Caribbean movies

Sex you don't see on TV

"Sex you don't see on TV", is my next book, which is scheduled to be published soon; make sure you get a copy. This work was designed to make your love life more pleasurable, and reduce the difficulties that are so common in couples who are laid back or lack sexual imagination. In this book we take a look at the advantages and disadvantages (if any) of each position for excitement, erection, and orgasm. Please note that the advantages that each variant brings are diverse, but on the other hand they are not intended to be used to convert the act to a laboratory for sexual techniques. They are geared to broaden your imagination and make you get your groove back, more so taking your love life from stale to exquisite, taking you from boring to irresistible. It is not my objective to portray the sex act as a mechanical process, where some say sex becomes like mathematics, you + (add) passion, you − (subtract) the clothes, you ÷ (divide) the legs and if you are lucky, you 'x' (multiply) the eggs.

We know sex is not divorced from other components such as, emotions, security, love, compassion and benevolence, and goes a long way in enhancing the dynamics of the relationship. I intentionally omitted naming these positions, so as to demonstrate how un-limited they are. Every culture would have names for each position. What is important though is that they were selected as a guide to breaking the monotony and boredom (note I did not say in the bedroom as the bedroom should not be the only place where the act is performed). As it is often said, "when things get stale you have to shake it up", and keep reinventing yourself. So all of the husbands that have resisted my beckoning call, this one's for you, I'm here to help you spice it up, and change it up.

Acclaim for the Unapologetic Quest for Success

"A rarely universal book that unravels a cross-fertilization of two interesting cultures. It's riveting and merits a movie maybe "The Black Pearl of the Caribbean". I believe this has box office breaking potential". - Cephus Toney, Statistician.

"A master piece of Vincentian work. A book ahead of its time. I am sure there has never been anything like this before. It's gripping! A must read!" – Ophesta Stephens (unpublished poet)

"A very interesting story that captures and holds your attention all the way through... A book that will change your life forever. - Andra Layne (IT Specialist)

This would inspire anyone who may be daunted by social and economic circumstances; it shows what could be achieved through strong focus, sound discipline and unwavering perseverance".

A must read! – EB John, Kingstown, St. Vincent

An ideal collector's item. – Uriel Seaton, Head of security, Life-Line Medical Clinic

"A book with a difference. Twenty (20) years ahead of its time!" – Dr. Edmund Sealey (Former Chiropractor of the Victorious West Indies Cricket Team of the 80's)

I recommend this book highly; It is a well written account of the author's life. It is sure to inspire all its readers and possesses all the elements of an exciting hard to put down read........... – Kurt Bynoe, Marketing Consultant, St. Vincent and the Grenadines

Unapologetic Quest for Success... is a flamboyantly crafted retrospection of an audacious young man's pathway to the fulfillment of his dream. It also, provides helpful insights and inspirations on the essentials of real life *"lucha"* in achieving such success. -Ezra D. Ledger, Chemical Engineer

A book written in the Caribbean by a Caribbean man, backed by a Caribbean woman, about Caribbean lands for the world to enjoy. An 'uncopiable' style by an interestingly unique author, an 'un-put-downable' read. – Clara Delia Breto, Chile

Highly readable…. A marvelous introduction to Vincentian and Cuban culture, and also alternative medicine. – Nicole John, Montreal Canada.

An exceptional book! Your story and poetry are essentially Caribbean, but your message is universal. Your ideas are profound, to the point and easy to read. You can be classified not only as a top class physician but also a prolific writer and poet. – John James – patient, London, U. K.

"Two books for the price of one! The epic story is the unvarnished truth of the life history of a rural boy of genuinely "humble" beginning; who survived some of the most atrocious and devious events of life struggles, including a most heinous attempt of homicide against the lives of his entire family; but who still grew up to become a medical doctor associated with international record breaking fame, thus becoming one of the most illustrious and popular icons in his country.

The Unapologetic quest for success is a read for all; however it is the fervent wish of the author that this story will serve as an inspiration beacon for all those youths who would share similar life experiences to his.

The book is an emotion-packed read. Despite the authentic nature of the story the contents of its chapters are pregnant with the sort of excitements and mood swings that I am sure would keep its readers glued to its pages. His poetic side complements the story but also brings out the deeper thoughts of the author. A must read! – Ardon Nelson, poet, song writer, literary and performing arts critic, consultant in urban planning, St. Vincent and the Grenadines.

A stunningly awesome piece of Caribbean work. It is pregnant with intellectual contents that make you hold the author in awe. It is flinchingly emotional, candid and at times satirical and epigrammatic with a dash of humor and symbolism. Translated from Spanish – Maria Hidalgo Perez, Lawyer, Havana, Cuba.

Bibliography

a. Adams, Edgar (1996) 'Linking the Golden Anchor with the Silver Chain'.

b. Jet Magazine, September 8th, 2008

c. National Geographic / China – Inside the Dragon Special Issue May 2008

d. Reid, Daniel (1989) 'The Tao of Health, Sex and Longevity', Simon & Schuster.

e. Schnabl, Siegfried (1978 Edition) 'El Hombre y la Mujer en la Intimidad'.

f. Strouts, A. F, Yarnelle, E. J., Hood, R. V., Clark, J. R. and Presser, S. R. (1969) 'Mathematics II', John Wiley & Sons Inc.

g. St. Vincent and the Grenadines Ministry of Tourism travel magazine (Ins and Out 2008

h. St. Vincent and the Grenadines Tourism website (http://www.svgtourism.com)

Printed in the United States
by Baker & Taylor Publisher Services